Learn to Draw with
Chappy the Chipmonk

Medieval Fantasy

MICHAEL GUGLIOTTO

Dedicated to my mother who once said
"An artist can see beauty in a mud puddle."

Copyright © 2020 by Michael Gugliotto
Illustrations copyright © 2020 by Michael Gugliotto

All rights reserved. This book, or parts thereof,
may not be reproduced in any form without permission.

www.chappythechipmonk.com

ISBN: 978-1-6752-2551-6

Printed in the USA

TABLE OF CONTENTS

MATERIAL LIST 5
WHAT YOU SHOULD KNOW BEFORE YOU START 6

Learn to Draw

MEDIEVAL KNIGHT 10
CASTLE PARTS 16
CASTLE 22
PRINCESS 30
DRAGON 36
SWORD IN STONE 40
WIZARD 44
JOUSTING KNIGHT 50
OGRE 60
KING 64

Secrets of Drawing Better

1 Drawing Simple Shapes 14
2 Blind Contour Drawing 15
3 Vase Face Illusion 20
4 Still Life Window Matte Drawing 28
5 Upside Down Drawing 34
6 Yarn Hair Face Drawing 42
7 Self Portrait 48
8 Stained Glass Tracing 49
9 Grid Drawing 54
10 Chappy's Flash Card Shapes 68
11 Flip Chip Book 71

CHAPPY'S EXTRAS 76

A note from the author

What I found out about most step by step books, is that they do not consider the drawing development stages of children, and therefore fail in there attempt to teach them how to draw. As an art teacher, what I know as one of the biggest hurdles children have, along with shape relationships, is drawing proportions. In this book I have many methods that overcome this hurdle, including a simple folding paper technique. Another method I use, is focusing on simple shapes. Included in the book is my *Secrets for Drawing Better*, that I have developed through many years of experience. Not only, is this book a step by step book, it also dives into cognitive concepts and methods to improve your drawing skills. I hope you enjoy this book and have fun drawing.

Hi boys and girls my name is Chappy, Chappy the chipmonk and I want to help you learn how to draw. By following my easy step by step book you will greatly improve your drawing skills. Let's get started.

You will find that this book is best suited if your age level is between 8-12 years old or if you are in the grades 2nd to 6th. Each drawing activity has a suggested level.

Each project will tell you the materials you will need. You might ask, what a material is? A material is something you need to use in order to make your project, like a pencil or eraser. Here is a list of all the basic materials you will need for the whole book.

- ❏ Pencils
- ❏ Paper
- ❏ Crayons or markers for coloring in drawings
- ❏ Drawing Board - Ask your parents if they can buy one at the art store or to save money you can do what I do. Get a piece of Masonite board from your local building supply store (this board is great since it is smooth, rigid, and lightweight). Cut it down to 14" x 20" for 12" x 18" paper, or 11" x 14" for 9" x 12" paper. Sometimes they will cut it for you if you ask them nicely.
- ❏ Flash light or small lamp
- ❏ Eraser
- ❏ Graph Paper
- ❏ Masking or Artist Tape (looks like masking tape but it is white, buy at any art supply store)
- ❏ Oak Tag or thin cardboard
- ❏ Scissors
- ❏ Glue
- ❏ Yarn
- ❏ Ruler
- ❏ Colored Chalk
- ❏ Tracing Paper

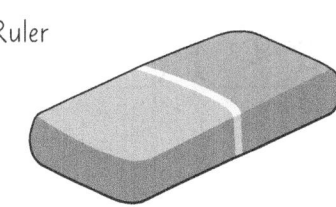
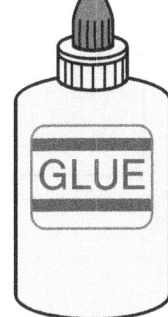

Drawing Board sizes

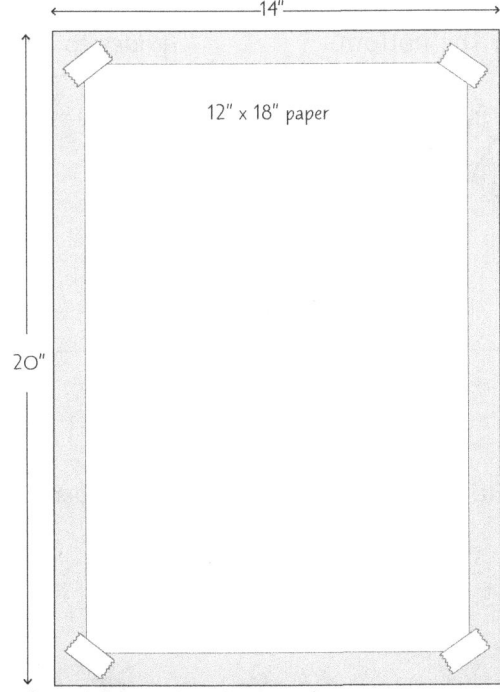
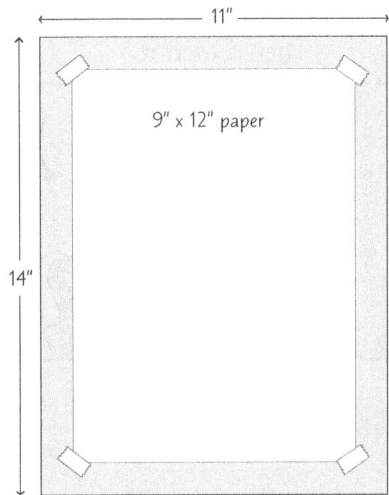

In this book we will only be using 9" x 12" as the largest paper size

Here's what you should know Before you start

Many activities in this book fold paper, to use as guides when drawing. Here are instructions on how to do it:

Step 1: start with your flat sheet of paper.

Step 2: Fold in Half.

Step 3: Fold in Half again.

 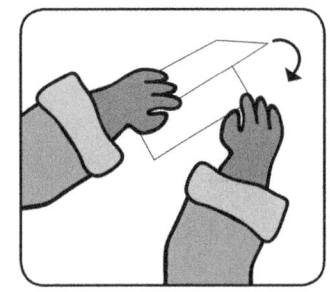  

Step 4: Open paper to see fold marks.

Step 5: Fold the top of the paper to the middle. Then Open it.

Step 6: Do the same for the bottom.

Done: Now you have fold marks to use as guides to help you draw.

   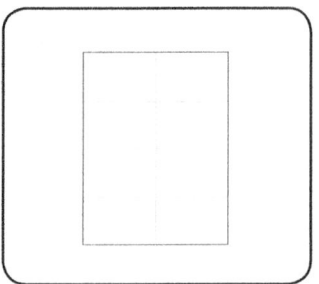

 You can also watch the Paper folding online video at www.chappythechipmonk.com/paperfolding

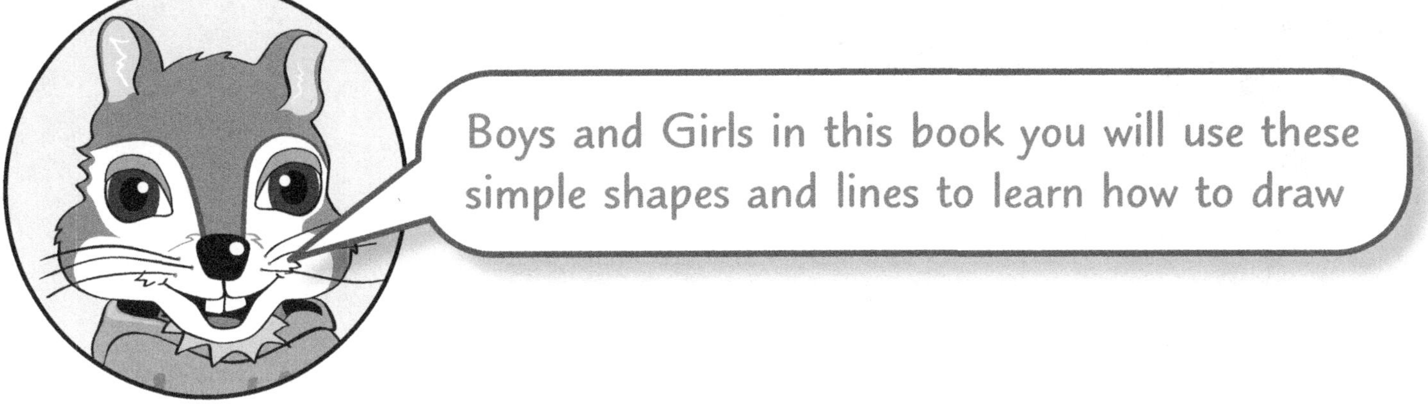

Boys and Girls in this book you will use these simple shapes and lines to learn how to draw

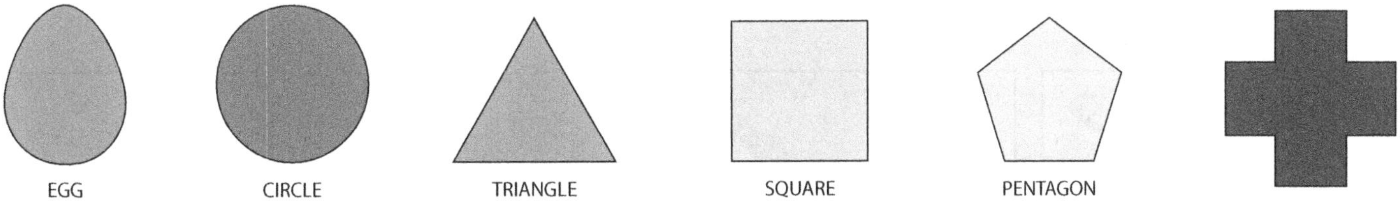

EGG CIRCLE TRIANGLE SQUARE PENTAGON CROSS

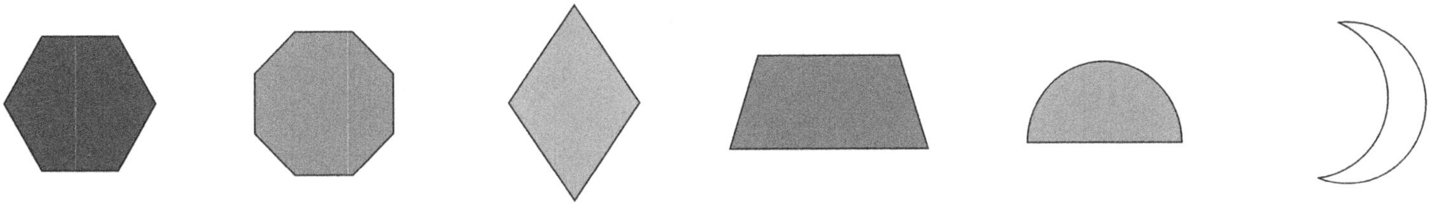

HEXAGON OCTAGON DIAMOND TRAPEZOID HALF CIRCLE CRESCENT MOON

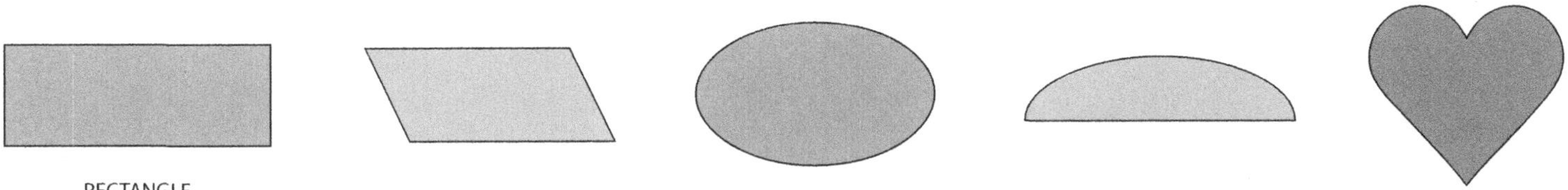

RECTANGLE PARALLELOGRAM OVAL HALF OVAL HEART

Zig Zag

Curvy

Wavy

Curved

Wiggly

Curly

Parallel

When drawing always draw lightly at first so you can easily erase. Then you can later darken in the lines you want to keep. This is what Artist's do all the time.

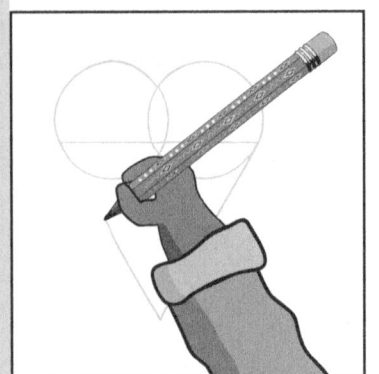 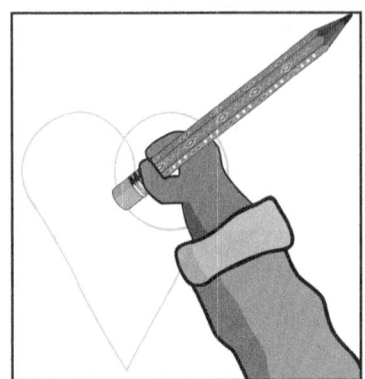 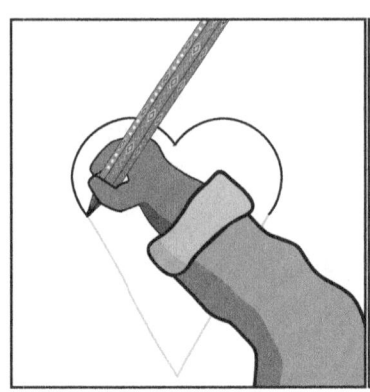 

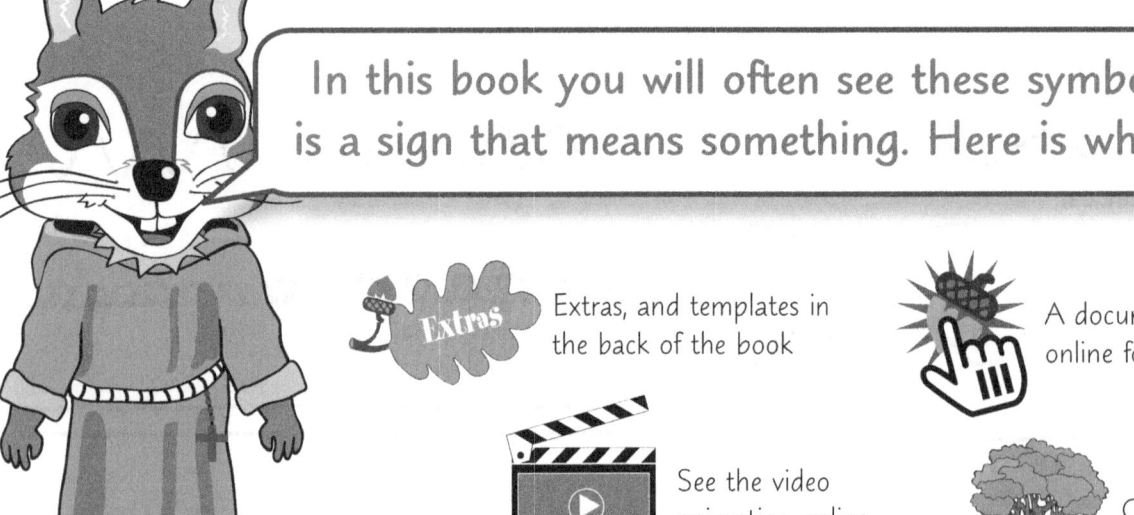

In this book you will often see these symbols. A symbol is a sign that means something. Here is what they mean.

Extras, and templates in the back of the book

A document that is available online for printing

See the video animation online

Comments for parents

Erase lines you don't need

Drawing tip

Note to parents:

I designed this book for elementary aged school children to learn how to draw by following along with Chappy the Chipmonk. Most of the activities are easy step by step follow along instructions that your child will be able to do by themselves with minimal help from you. But there are times when they will need help and this is why I am writing to you. As a previous art teacher I know that drawing is a very important outlet for children to express their feelings and emotions. If this outlet is not properly guided by putting too many restricted adult art rules, it could work the opposite way and diminish their artistic development. Positive input is greatly needed for artistic success. So here are some helpful hints when helping or giving instructions. Remember always in children's art it is the artistic experience and process that is most important, not the final product. I don't know how to stress this enough. By giving praise to their art work no matter how it looks will greatly increase your child's value and help them learn. Since children are so creative there is no need to lie. Only choose something you like about their drawing and comment on it. Perhaps you like the way they drew a nose or ears. Even if you do find something out of place, you can cunningly choose your praise. For example you could say "that is a very interesting color you used for the tigers stripes" even though it might be green. If you ask them why they chose that color, I think you will get some very uncommon answers, that may help you understand your child better. Children between the ages of seven and nine are in the schematic stages of artistic development. They are still processing symbols that they use to interpret the world around them. You may have noticed that your son or daughter draws a person the same way. The face of a man or woman will have the same style using the same mouth, nose or eyes for both. They may draw a house the same way every time. These schemes should not be discouraged but instead nurtured and guided towards different variations. What I mean, is if your child is drawing the same nose on each person every time, you could suggest different ways to draw a nose. The struggle between drawing rules and creativity is a very fine line. Just remember, when you see your child struggling or frustrated, give them other suggestions to help guide them through the artistic process. Be patient, reflect that nothing can be done overnight, and by practicing every day your skills will gradually improve. By following these hints and doing the activities in the book, they will greatly receive the valuable tools necessary for their drawings to succeed and flourish in the future.

Learn to Draw
Medieval Knight

Difficulty: Level 2

Materials Needed: 8 1/2" x 11" paper, pencil, eraser.

When we draw the knight let us think about what he stands for. Along with protecting the kingdom a knight took a code of chivalry. That was an unwritten form of conduct, such as bravery, courtesy, honor and great gallantry toward women.

Step 1

Let's look for some simple shapes in the Knight with Sword. I see rectangles (#1), a half circle (#2), a hexagon (#3), circle shapes (#4), triangle (#5), and an oval (#6).

Step 2

Fold your paper into 8 sections. Refer to page 6 or watch the online video at www.ChappytheChipmunk.com/paperfolding

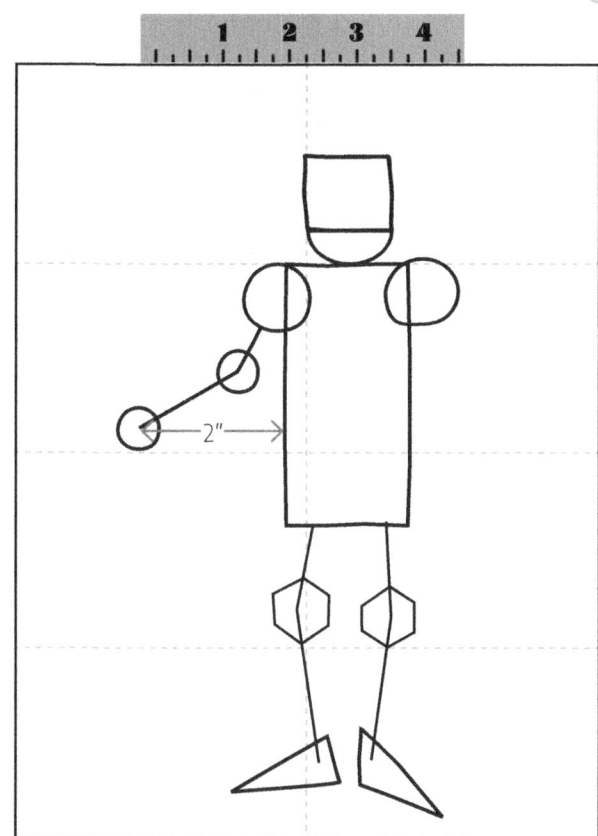

Step 3

One method to drawing a person is to start out with what's called a stick figure. For the joints like elbows and knees we usually use circles or squares but for the knees we are going to use an hexagon since he is wearing armor and it already looks like a hexagon. Make sure you get the measurements right and lined up to your fold marks. For example the bottom of the head rests on the 1st fold mark and the bottom of the knees are near the 3rd fold mark. Use a ruler if you need to. This step is important since it outlines the size and proportion you will be drawing at.

Step 4

Now lets use some more shapes for the sword and shield. Both forms are basically a rectangle and triangle put together. Make sure the top of your sword is aligned with the top of the head. To make the arms, connect the outside of the circles with lines. Do the same with the hexagon of the legs. Use two rectangles as a cross shape for the helmet and a wavy line and oval for the top. Pay careful attention to where things intercept.

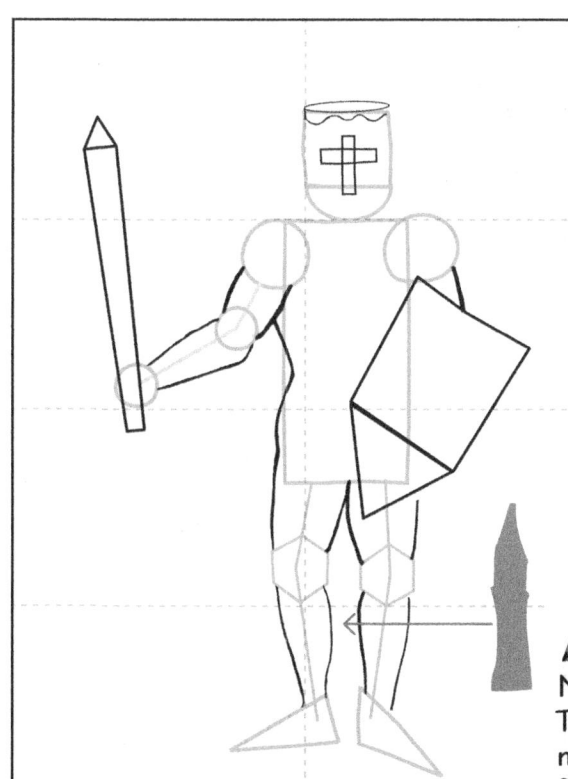

Tip

Notice this shape. This is what you call negative space. Always look for shapes like these since it will help you to draw.

Your doing great!

Learn to Draw
Knight continued

Step 5

Add the sword bottom detail. The shapes I see are half circles and curvy lines. Continue to add more details to the right arm and shoulder. For the head, go over with your pencil to define the helmet more and add some half circles on the cross design and rectangles for the eyes. Lets also add a rectangle cross shape for the shield and make the outside more curvy. Notice the placement for the cross is on the middle fold mark and near the top of the triangle. Add more lines for the feet and also make them and the knees more curvy. Now would be a good time to erase some lines you don't need.

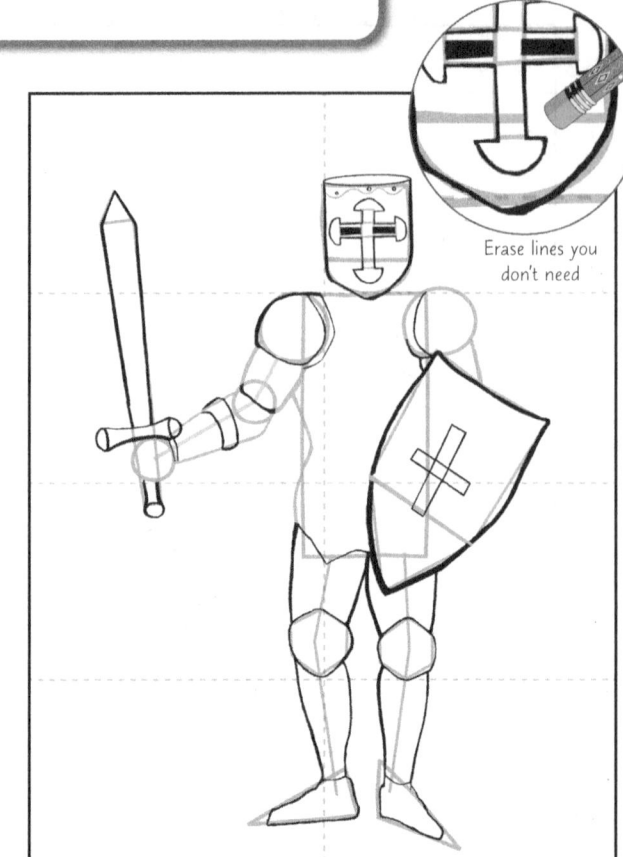

Erase lines you don't need

Step 6

This is what we have after we erased the lines we didn't need. Lets work on the hand. Hands are the most difficult part of the body to do. So if you are having trouble do not be discouraged. Artist's always have trouble drawing hands. Within the circle you made, draw 4 rectangles with curved ends to the center of the circle with the top finger being slightly larger. Look at your own fingers to get size relationships. Fingers have 3 parts. We are only drawing one part right now. Next make the shoulders more curvy and draw the collar. Draw the rest of the details. Did you notice some parallel lines?

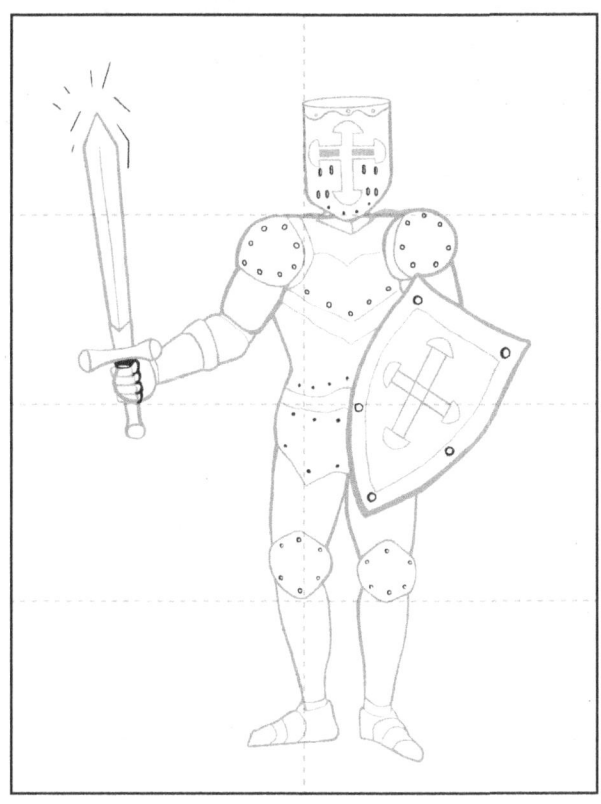

 **Step 7**

Let's finish the hand, by drawing the other part of the fingers. Draw in the holes and rivets of the armor. Draw one side of the rivet or hole thicker and darker. This will give it more of a real look.

 **Step 8**

Erase the lines you don't need. Make some lines thicker or darker to make your drawing look good.

Faith is our shield, righteousness our breastplate, salvation our helmet, and spirit our sword. Use them against evil.

Secrets of How to Draw Better

Drawing Simple Shapes

Boys and girls to help you draw better it helps to practice drawing these simple shapes below. More are in the back of the book. Trace on the dotted line.

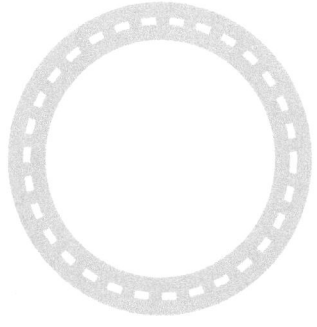      

CIRCLE   TRIANGLE   SQUARE

Using the space below, practice drawing the shapes

   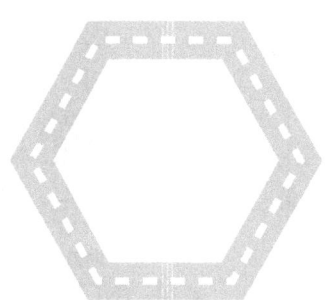   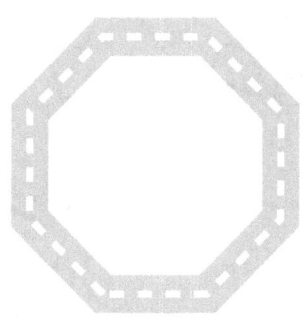

PENTAGON   HEXAGON   OCTAGON

14

Secrets of How to Draw Better
Blind Contour Drawing

Difficulty: Level 3

We are going to draw an object without looking at our paper. Sounds crazy doesn't it? But this will actually help our drawing skills and teach us how to see more detail. Since our drawing will look like nothing that we are trying to draw, We don't have to worry about how our drawing will look. That will be fun!

Materials Needed: pencil, eraser, white paper or drawing pad, drawing board, masking or artist tape, towel, timer.

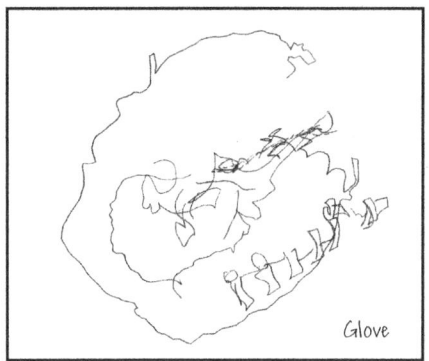
Glove

Step 1

Take an object you like. Make sure the object you pick has detail in it, for example if you like baseball pick a baseball glove that has lots of detail instead of a baseball or bat that doesn't have much detail. Once you have your object picked place it in front of you. Take a sheet of white paper, and tape it down on a board so it doesn't move, or use a drawing pad.

Step 2

Hold your pencil over the paper ready to draw. Now put a towel over your drawing hand and paper so you can't see it. Look at the object closely. Pretend that you are touching a specific spot of the object. Pretend you are following the line of the object with your pencil inch by inch. Start drawing that line without lifting your pencil. Do not look at your paper until you are finished. Use a timer set for 3 minutes.

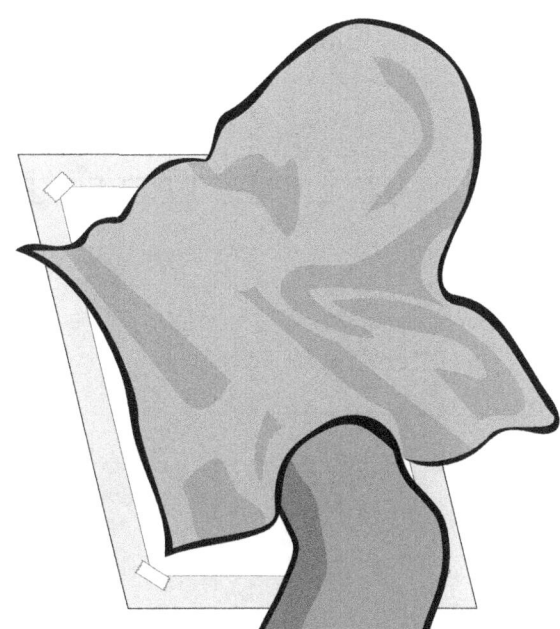

Parents: By looking more closely at an object our minds begin to see more details and it teaches us that lines can be expressive.

Learn to Draw
Castle Parts

Difficulty: Level 2

Later in the book we will draw a whole castle. But, before we do, let's learn some valuable ways to help us.

Materials Needed: pencil, eraser, ruler, graph paper (1/4" scale).

Patterns

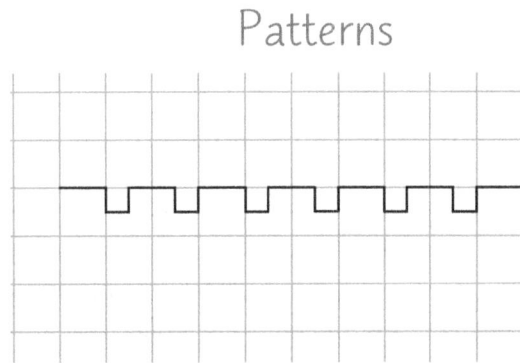

🍂 Castle Wall Tops

Take a sheet of graph pager. We are going to practice drawing the wall tops of castles. They are called the Merlon (the wall part) and Embrasure (the opening). We can make them any size but let's do a small size of a half graph square each.

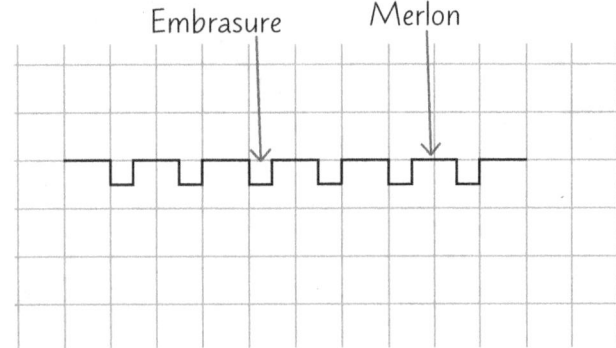

Embrasure   Merlon

Next make another one a little bigger. One graph square wide by a half graph box high. Same height just wider.

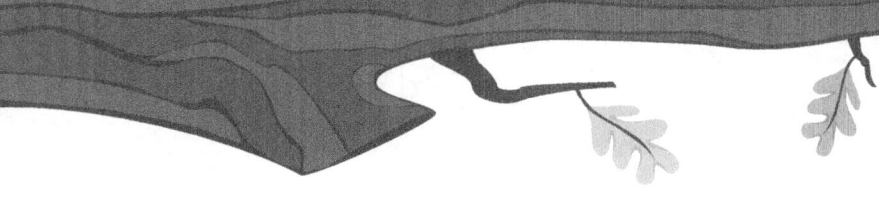

Now were going to make some arch stone work for our castle. Once again, we can make them any size. The important thing is to follow the same pattern. We are going to start our arch unit with a straight line a quarter graph square wide and draw the arch a half a graph square wide by a half graph square high.

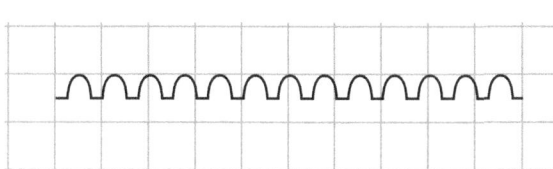

Put them together to get this. Don't worry If you draw some bigger or smaller. The graph paper is only a guide. Heres another one below that is bigger. See if you can draw it.

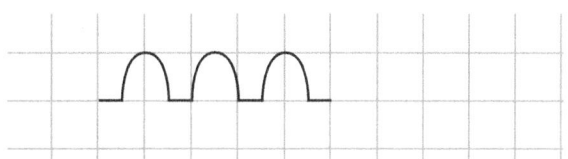

Castle Turret Parts

Just like wall tops, we are going to draw a line that goes up straight and down in a pattern. However, this time we are going to make the outside merlons smaller than the inside. This will make your turret look curved without making any curved lines.

Tower top

 ### Step 1

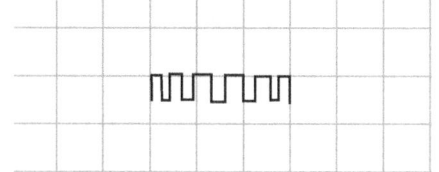

 ### Step 2

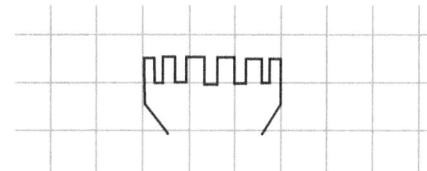

Step 3

Draw the bottom arches starting from the center dotted line. These arches are a little higher and squished from the others that you drew earlier. Notice they are symmetrical.

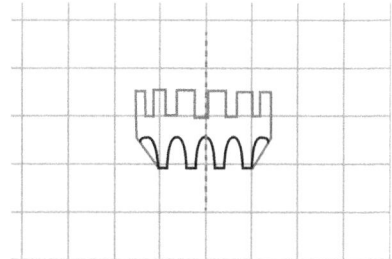

Learn to Draw
Castle Parts continued

Turret Banister

 **Step 1**

For the railing banister draw an upside down trapezoid. The dotted line shows you how symmetrical it is (do not draw it).

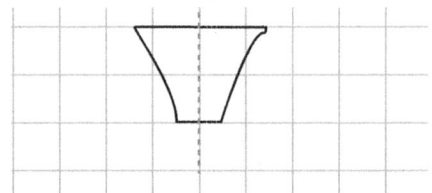

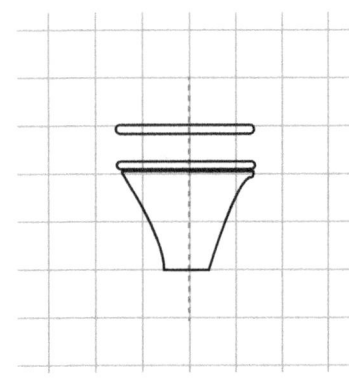

 **Step 2**

Draw 2 narrow rectangles with curved sides on the top.

 **Step 3**

Draw a Big W for the bottom with curved lines and connect the curved rectangles you made with straight lines. For the railings draw rectangles for the openings with the bigger one in the center.

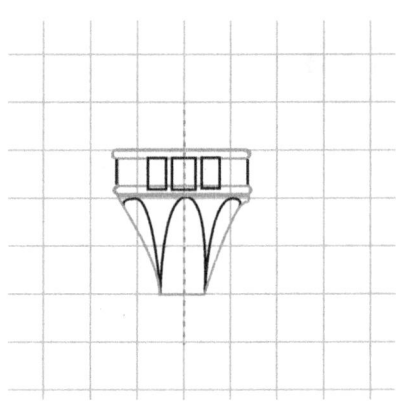

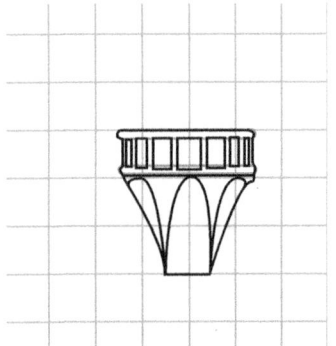

 **Step 4**

Finish the banister by drawing more narrow rectangles. Make each rectangle from the center narrower than the next. This will make your turret look like it's curved without drawing curved lines. Neat trick!

 # Castle Chain

 ## Step 1

Draw a oval on an angle.

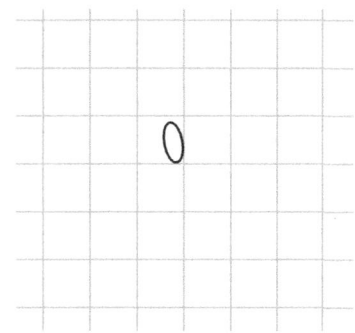

 ## Step 2

Draw another one overlapping the first.
Continue making ovals until it looks like a chain

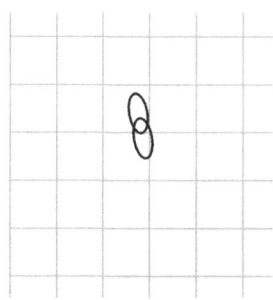

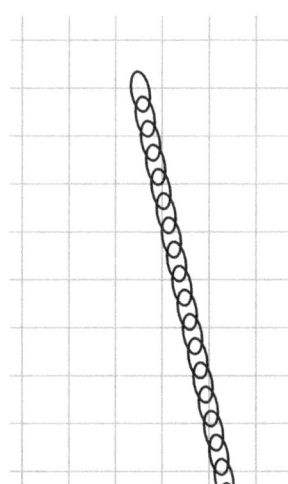

The person who asks a question is a fool for a minute, the person who does not ask is a fool for life.

Secrets of How to Draw Better
 ## Vase Face Illusion

Difficulty: Level 2

What we are going to do boys and girls is trace the shadow profile of a persons face.

Materials Needed: pencil, eraser, 9 x 12 white and 12 x 18 black paper, another person, flashlight or small lamp, ruler, colored chalk, masking or artist's tape, scissors, glue, blank wall.

 Step 1

Sit the person next to an empty wall and shine a lamp or flashlight on them so you can see their profile shadow on the wall. It doesn't need to be a very bright light so a flashlight would work just fine. Make sure you sit the person sideways so you can see their profile.

Step 2

Fold the short side of your paper in half and open it. Position and tape your paper on the wall where the shadow of the persons profiled face falls. Also make sure to line up the profile shadow on one side of the paper an inch or so away from the fold mark and not in the center.

Step 3

Now take your pencil and trace the profile. After you are done take a ruler and draw a line on the top and bottom of your tracing.

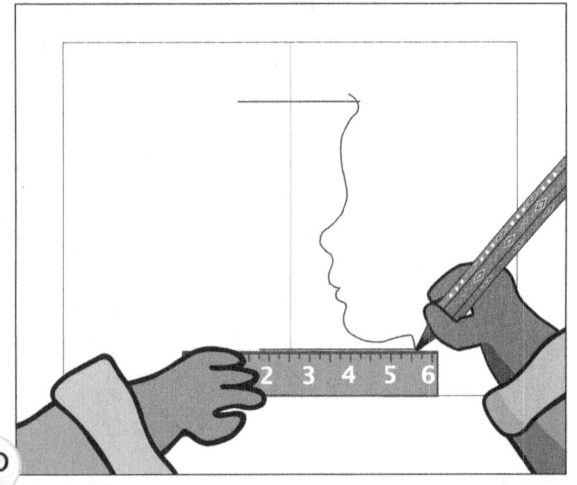

Step 4

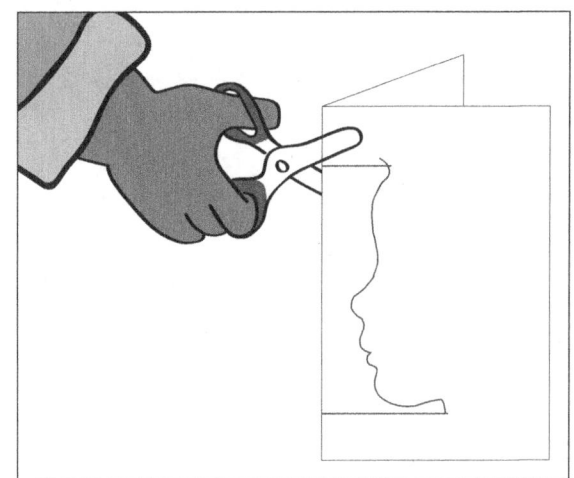

Fold you paper in half so you can see the pencil lines and cut it out. (For older children: Instead of folding and cutting your profile out, try to draw the same profile on the opposite side of the fold mark in the same position then cut it out. You may find this challenging, and you will need to use your eraser a lot, but it will greatly improve your drawing skills.) Now you have what looks like a vase.

Step 5

Take your vase shape and paste it on the bottom half of your black 12 x 18 paper. Now you can draw in some flowers at the top of your vase. Look at your vase on the black paper and you will notice that it also looks like two faces looking at each other.

> An orchid in a deep forest sends out its fragrance even if no one is around to appreciate it.

Parents: There is a certain part of the brain that controls creativity and drawing. If we tap into this and use this part of our minds we will be more successful. Because this activity focuses on the illusion: are we looking at a vase or two identical faces looking at each other? Our minds expand to meet its challenge, therefore increasing our drawing awareness. The use of symmetry helps us think about spaces differently. By drawing a side profile of the face, its proportions become familiar to us. For older children who choose to do the option mentioned above, their brains will get an extra work out. Just like in sports, we need to exercise certain muscles for improvement.

Learn to Draw
Castle

Difficulty: Level 2

Materials Needed: pencil, eraser, ruler, graph paper (1/4" scale).

The castle was a fortress to protect kings, nobles and family from their enemies. Build it well my friend.

 **Step 1**

Let's look for some simple shapes in the Castle. I see countless rectangles (#1), and squares (#2). I see circles (#3), half ovals (#4), and triangles (#5).

When you start don't forget to draw lightly so you can easily erase.

Hint — Use a ruler to draw straight lines

Step 2

On your graph paper start your first tower 3 graph squares in from the right edge of the paper and 3 graph squares up from the bottom. Make the base of the tower 12 graph squares high by 5 graph squares wide. Count how many graph squares you need for other shapes. The windows are half graph squares. Make a smaller rectangle inside the window and shade it in. This will give it some dimension.

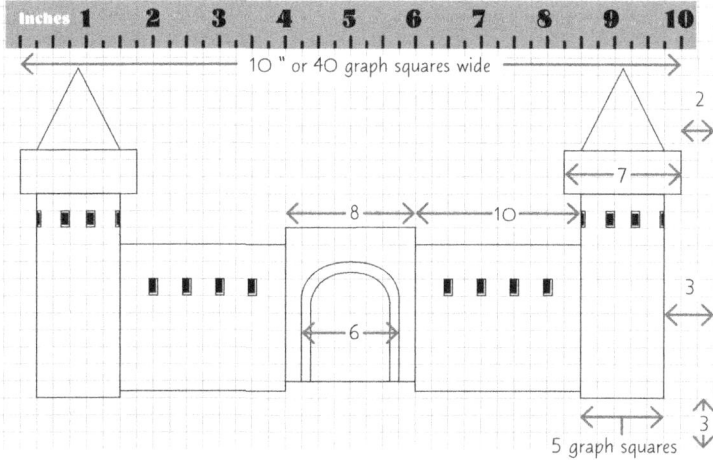

Step 3

Next fill in the details and erase the lines that we don't need from step 2. See *Learn to Draw Castle parts* for ways to draw some of these items.

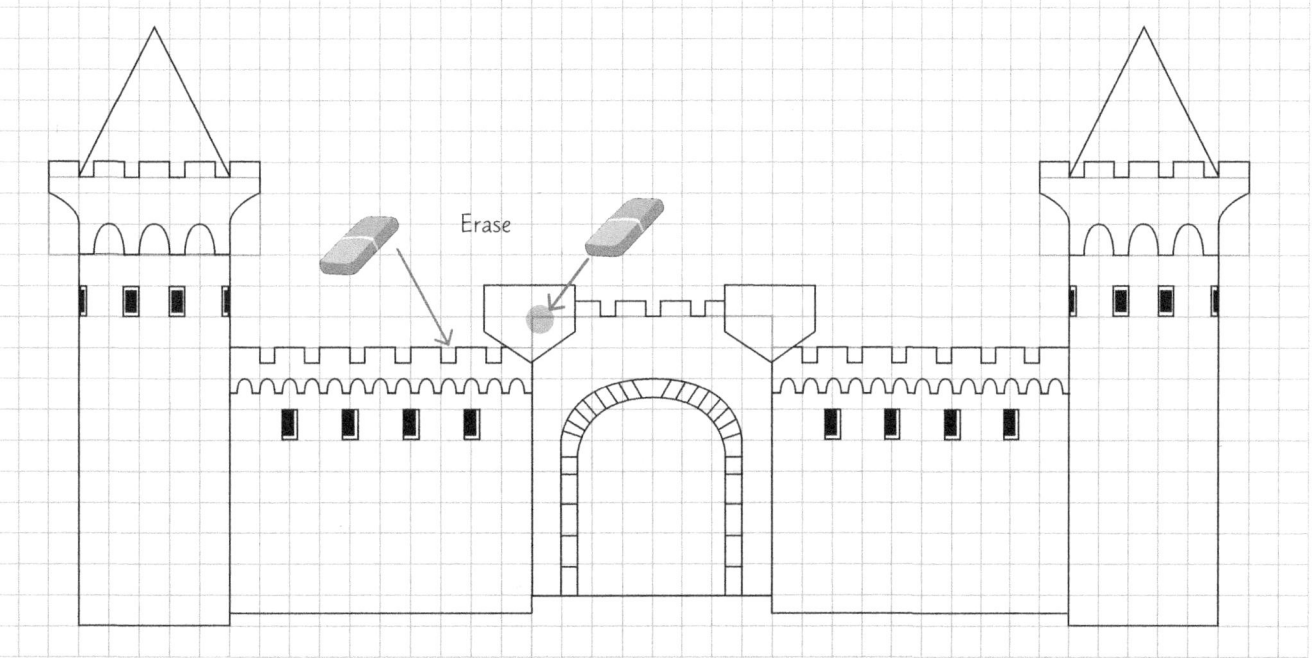

Learn to Draw

Castle continued

> Every truth has four corners: as a teacher I give you one corner, and it is for you to find the other three.

 **Step 4**

Draw more rectangles, triangles and circles at their correct graph square positions and graph square sizes. Sometimes there are half graph square sizes or shapes don't fit exactly. Don't worry the graph is only a guide. You are doing Great. Erase the lines that we don't need from step 3.

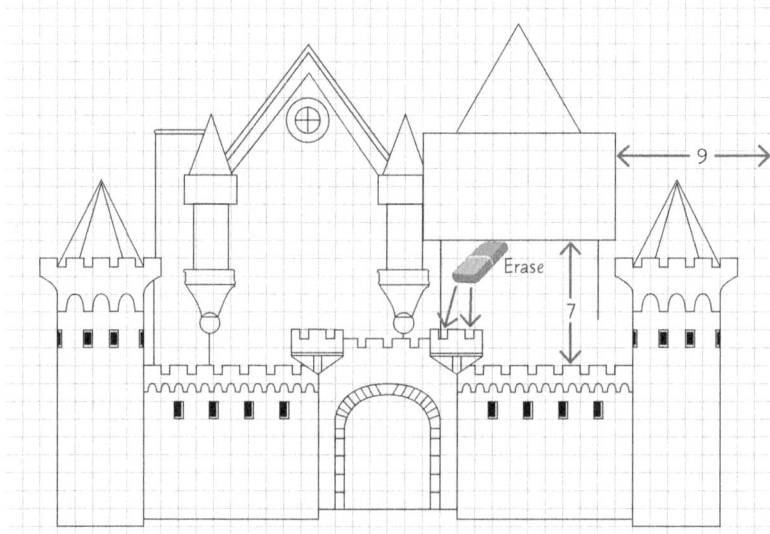

 **Step 5**

Continue measuring and drawing. See *How to Draw Castle Parts* for details. Erase all the lines that we don't need from step 4.

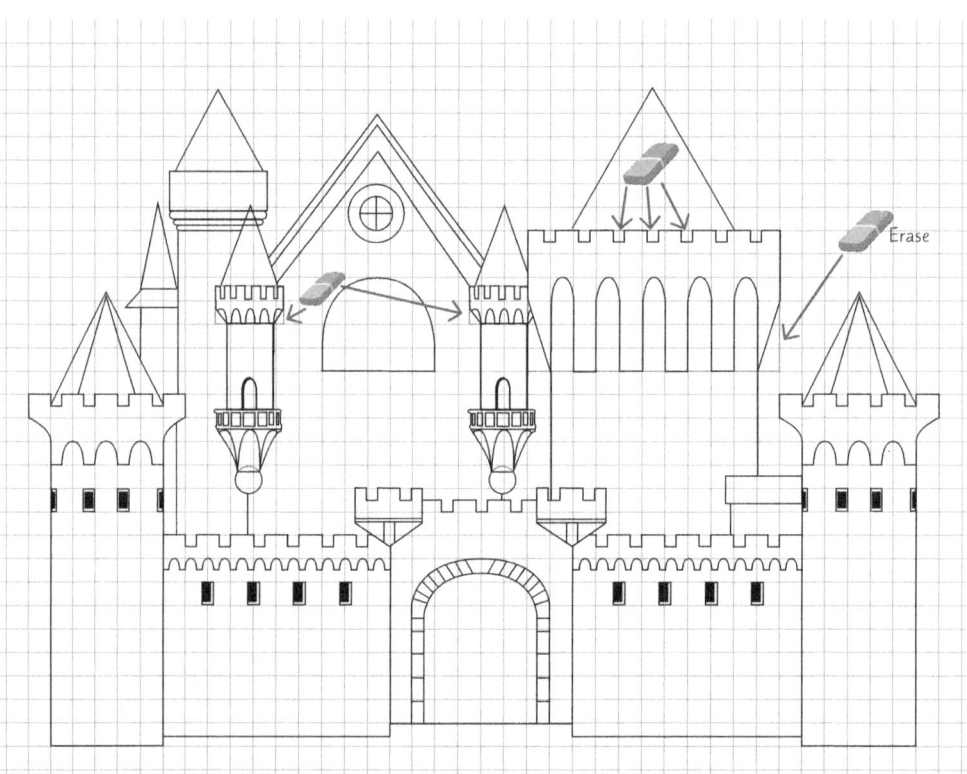

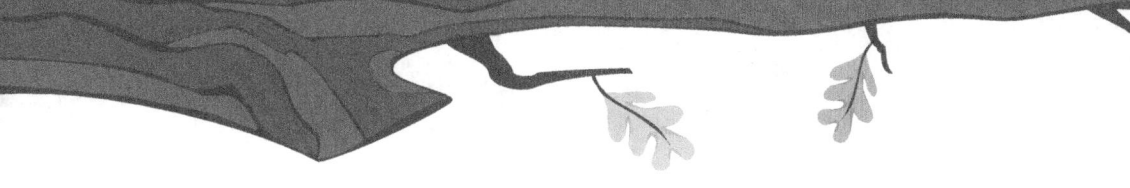

Step 6

Start to make the lines you keep darker. As you draw more and more you will begin to see the same patterns. Once you learn these patterns it will become more easy to draw and perhaps you will draw the pattern without the previous guides so you don't have to erase.

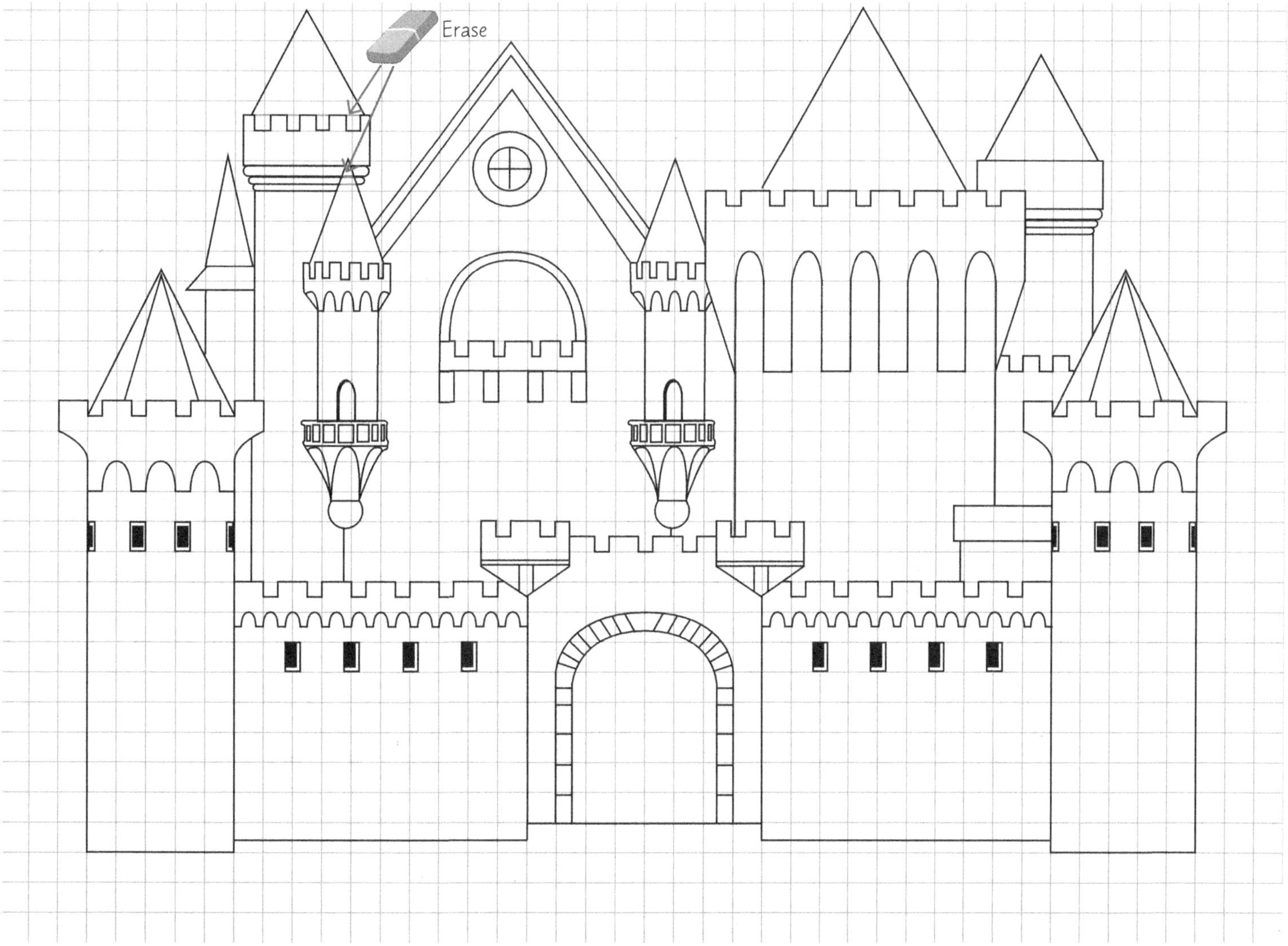

Erase

Learn to Draw

Castle continued

🌰 Step 7

Draw in more windows. Draw the left side of the windows with a thicker line or make it dark. This will give your castle a more realistic look.

Erase

Erase

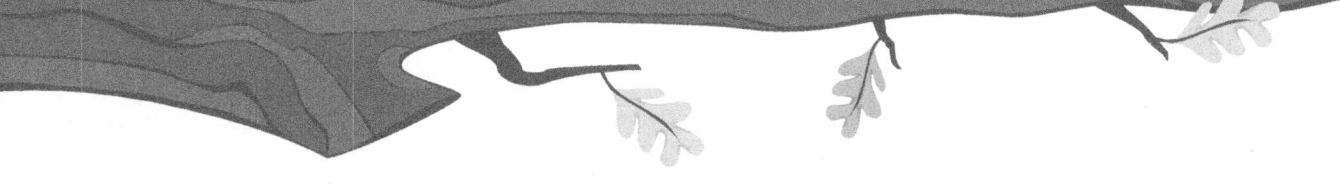

Step 8

Criss cross lines for the gate with dots on the ends. To draw the chain, it is just an oval that intersects. Use a dark upsidedown half moon shape in the two outside towers to give it dimension. Make some lines darker so objects look like they are in front of other objects. Finish the details and you are done!

Have fun living in your castle.

Dark Half Moon Shapes

27

Secrets of How to Draw Better
Still Life Window Matte Drawing

Difficulty: Level 2

Drawing from life is a wonderful secret that will help you draw better. By using my secret window matte from the back of the book you will be able to easily frame and focus in on what you are drawing. The widow matte has been used by many famous artist's including Michelangelo. Here's how it works.

Materials Needed: pencil, eraser, matte board or cardboard, scissors, ruler, toilet paper tube

Step 1

One of the biggest secrets to drawing is our knowledge of what's called positive and negative space. Positive space is the shape of any object in a picture. A few examples can be a baseball glove, a musical instrument, a bottle, a sand pail and shovel, a seashell, a pinwheel, a horse, a person, a dinosaur, a house, a chair, a teapot, a flower, a shamrock, a racing car, a fire engine, a train, and it can be anything. Negative space is the shape that is behind, around or in between positive shape objects in a picture. Let's look at an example. What is the positive space or shape in this picture. That's right the bike is the positive shape. What is the negative space? That's right. Any shape that is black.

Here are a few more pictures. Fill in the positive shapes with color and the negative space with black.

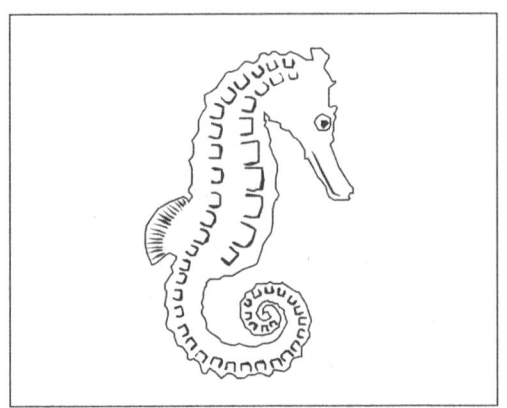

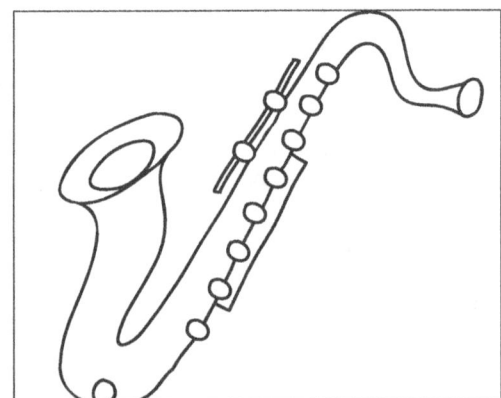

Step 2

Now we are ready to draw a still life but first we will need a window frame that we can make out of cardboard or matboard. Use my template in the back of the book and have your parents help you cut it out. To stand up our matte, I cut a recycled toilet paper tube in half, cut slits in it and slid them on the bottom of the matte so it stands.

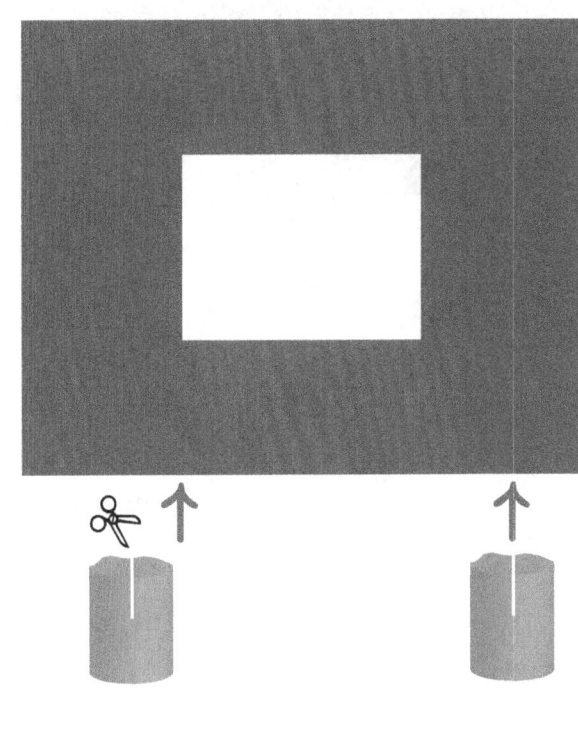

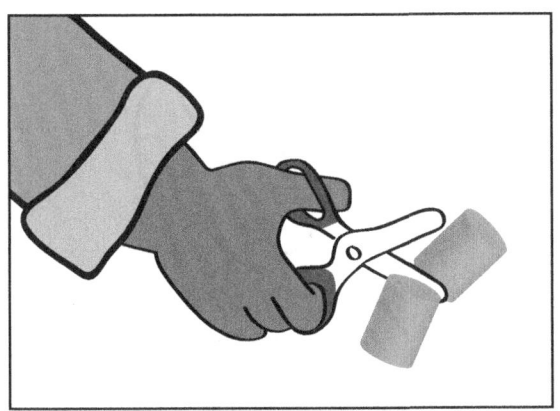

Step 3

Once you have your window matte take a few simple objects that you like. Maybe your favorite toy, a sand pail, a flower, a seashell, or a musical instrument. Arrange your object on an empty table with nothing around it. When we put your objects together we will have what artist's call a still life. Here's my still life example that I drew.

Step 4

Place the matte in front of your still life to frame your objects. Look for the positive and negative shapes and start drawing those shapes on a 9" x 12" sheet of paper. Another helpful secret is to try not to think of what the objects are when you're drawing, but just what there shapes are. Don't forget to combine simple shapes that you see to help you draw both the negative and positive spaces.

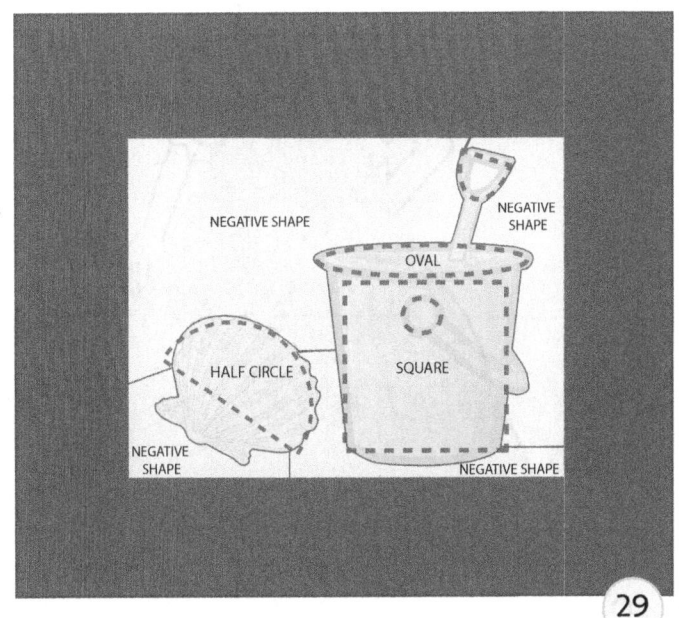

Learn to Draw
Princess

Difficulty: Level 2

Materials Needed: pencil, eraser, 8 1/2" x 11" paper.

A good princess is kind, loving and cares for her people. She represents innocence, mercy, peace, beauty and what is right and positive about the world.

 **Step 1**

Let's look for some simple shapes in the Princess. Diamonds shapes for diamonds in the crown (#1). That's easy. Half moons for some of the hair (#2). The letters B and D sideways for the lips. Letters are shapes too!(#3). Square for the body(#4) and ovals for the upper arms (#5). Don't forget the face, that's an oval too. Big Triangles for the dress (#6) and what shape is #7? You guessed it. Do you see any more simple shapes?

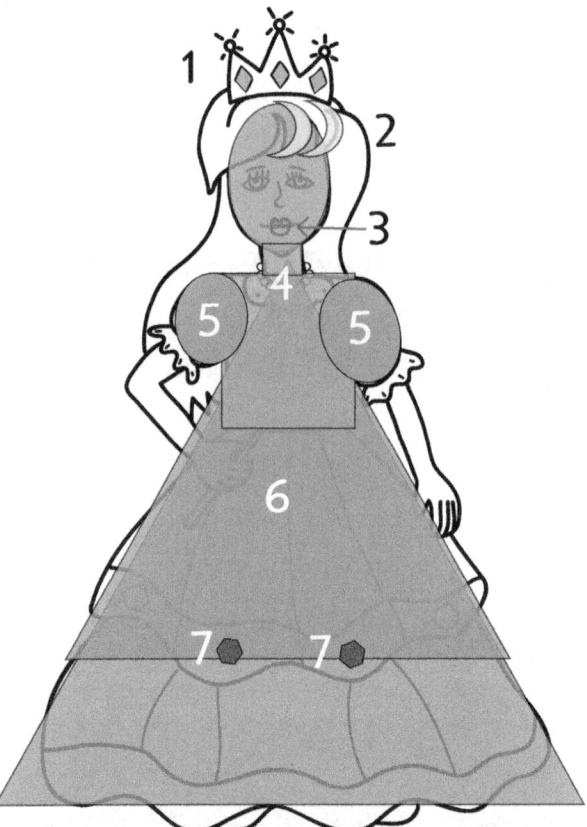

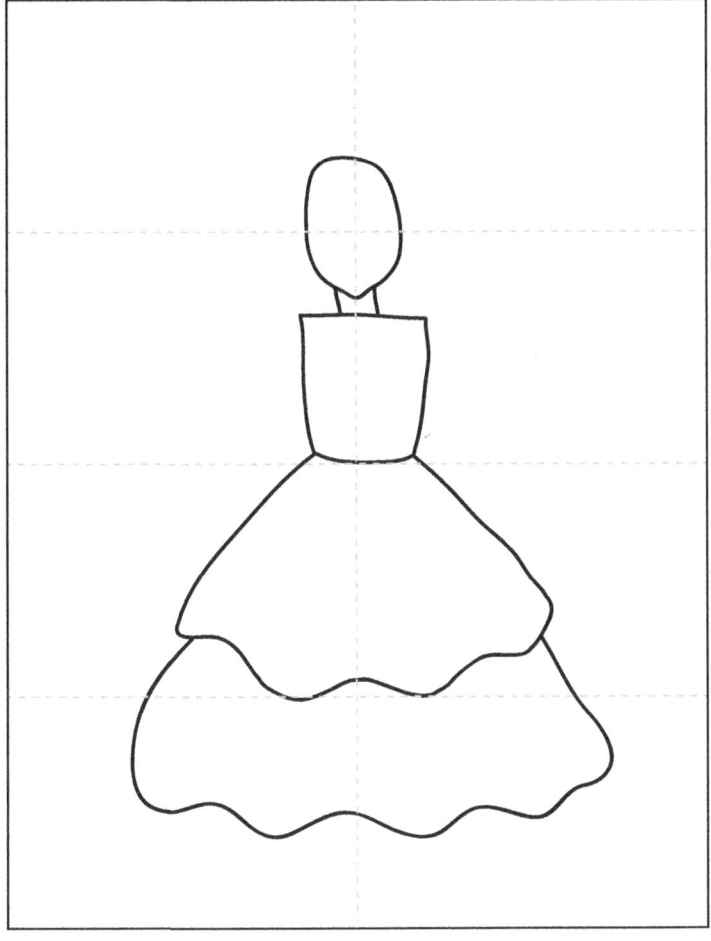

 ## Step 2

Take a blank sheet of 8 1/2" x 11" paper. Fold the paper in 8 sections as outlined on page 6 of this book. Next, draw an oval on the paper with the top center folds in the middle. Give the bottom of the oval a little point for the chin. Draw two small vertical lines for the neck and a square shape for the body. Make sure the bottom of the square is on the center fold mark. Next draw two overlapping triangles with squiggly lines on the bottom. Make sure you look at your fold marks and line up those triangle shapes.

  Don't be afraid to erase if things do not line up the first time.

Step 3

Let's draw the face. I like big eyes so let's draw some. Isn't it wonderful, the eyes go right on the folded line like two football shapes with circles in them. An upside down question mark for the nose or maybe a hook and lets not forget the capital letters "B" and "D" for the mouth with a line through them. Magnificent!

Learn to Draw
Princess continued

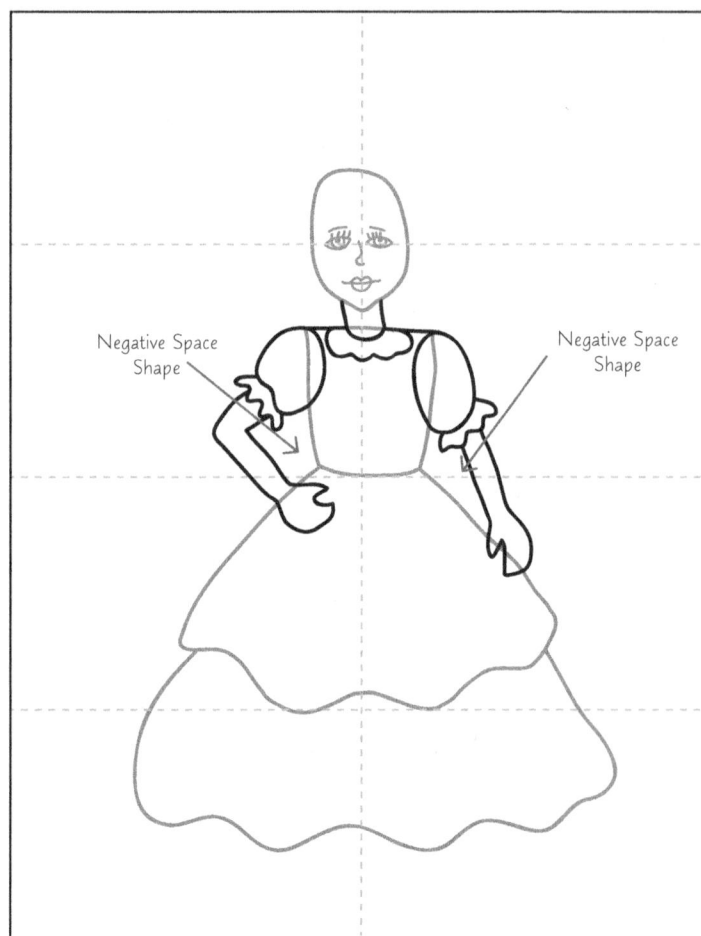

Step 4

How about some arms. Remember the ovals in step #1. Parallel lines for the rest of the arm and more ovals for the hands. Look at the negative space between the arms and body.

Erase the lines we don't need

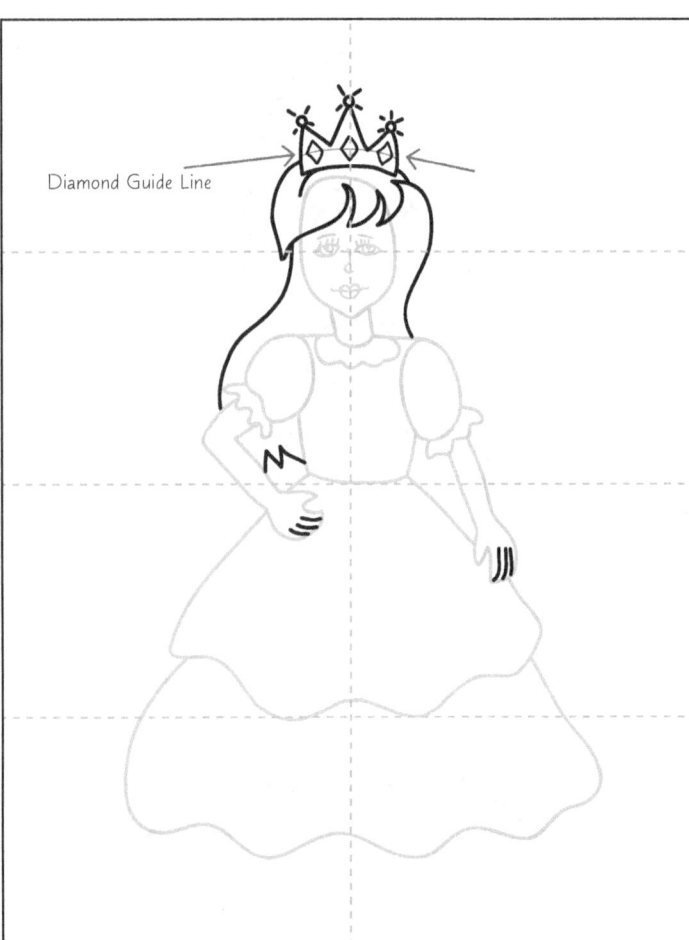

Step 5

I'm sick of this bald headed princess. Let's add some wavy hair. Remember the half moon shapes, and no princess is completer without a crown. For the diamonds I drew a curved guide line so each diamond shape would line up. Don't forget 3 lines for the fingers.

 **Step 6**

Let's draw some line decorations on the dress. Draw her necklace with circle shapes and finish the collar. Don't forget the shoes and add more details to the sleeves. That is looking great!

 **Step 7**

Now for the final touches. Let's draw the wand with some parallel lines, a big circle and some triangles. What do you call a six sided shape? Lets draw some of those to finish the dress.

 Erase the lines you don't need.

A heart set on love will do no wrong.

Secrets of How to Draw Better
Upside Down Drawing

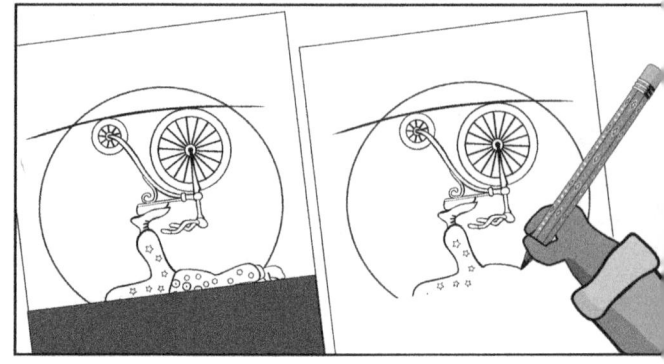

Difficulty: Level 3

Here's a nifty secret to help you to draw better, my way. Its called upside down drawing. No, you do not have to stand on your head and draw! Here's how it works.

Materials Needed: pencil, eraser, black paper, white paper.

Step 1

Use the picture on the opposite page. First take a colored sheet of paper, I like to use black but it can be any color and put it over the picture to reveal only the top part of the it.

Step 2

Take another sheet of white paper, start at the top and copy what you see. Don't move the black sheet until you have completely finished drawing that section.

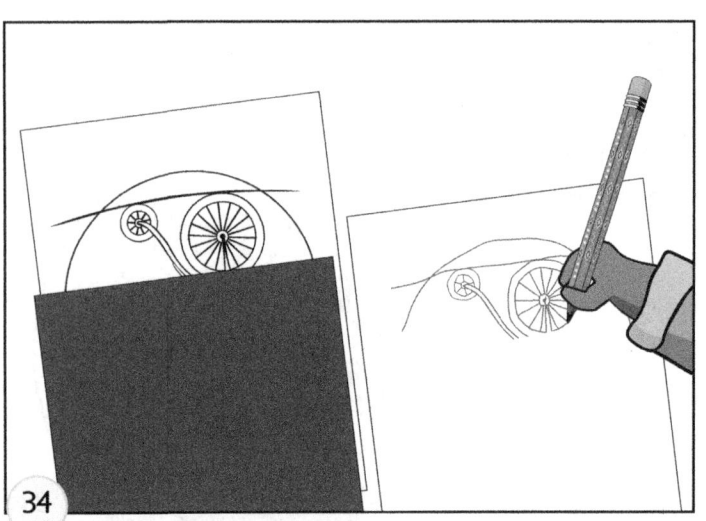

Step 3

Only After you've finished a section move the black sheet of paper that covers the drawing down a bit and continue drawing where you left off. Keep Doing this until your drawing is complete. Then turn your paper right side up to look at your drawing. How did you do?

 Parents: Our mind defines visual objects as symbols which usually get in the way when it comes to drawing. By drawing upside down we fool our minds into not using these visual symbols. By drawing the upside down image, our brain cannot focus on what we are drawing, but instead it more clearly focuses on shapes and their relationship to each other.

Learn to Draw Dragon

Difficulty: Level 3

Materials Needed: 9 x 12 sketch pad or paper, pencil, eraser.

The Dragon is the most feared beast for the knight. They are often said to have ravenous appetites and to live in caves, where they hoard treasure.

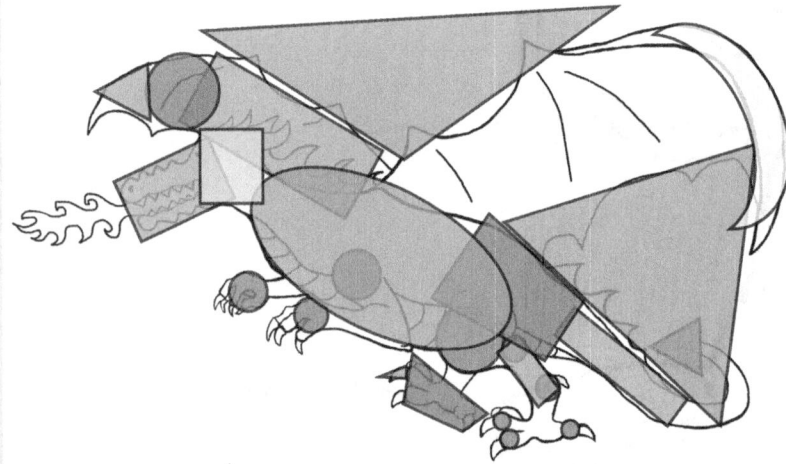

 **Step 1**

I can find many simple smaller shapes in the dragon and perhaps to many. These smaller shapes will not help when drawing his larger body. He is very curvy and we will have to rely on curved lines, negative shapes, and a wire frame to get started.

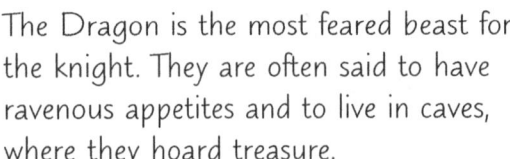 **Step 2**

Let's first fold our paper in 8 sections as outlined on page 6 of this book. Next from the center of the paper draw the curved lines for the wings. Note how far and where lines are in relation to the fold marks. Make sure when you draw the square for the head it is positioned on the 1st fold mark and the tail triangle is in the 8th folded section. Measure with a ruler if needed. If we get these proportions right then the rest will be easier.

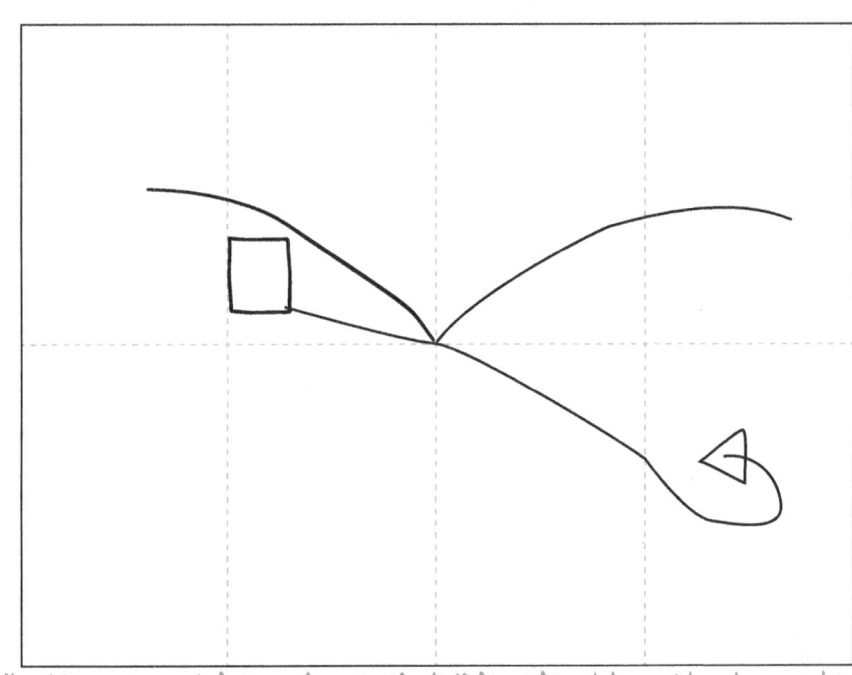

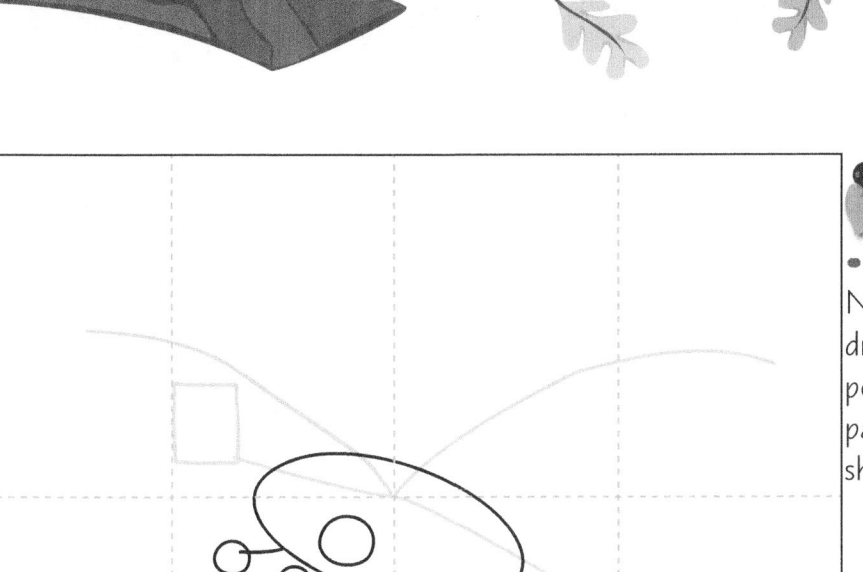

Step 3

Next, let's focus on the main body by drawing an oval and some circles for the position of the arms and legs. Once again, pay attention to how far and where the shapes and lines are placed.

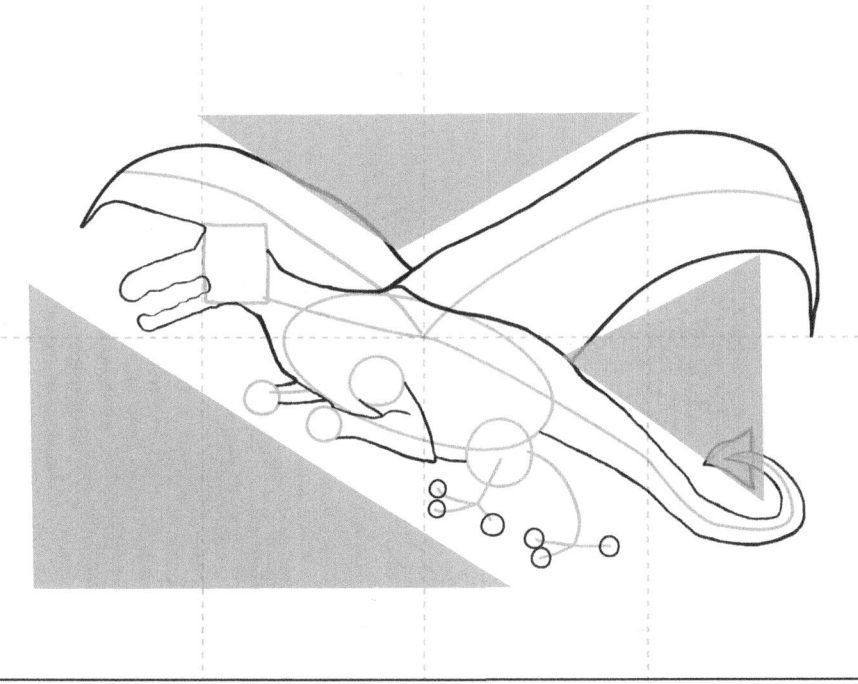

Step 4

Let's look at some negative shapes of the dragon. Do we see some triangles? We don't need to draw these but negative shapes help us see space relationships of positive shapes better. Continue to draw new lines and connect them as you see in this drawing.

Learn to Draw

Dragon continued

🌰 Step 5

Let's connect those circle shapes and draw the back feet. Look at the negative shapes shown and where they are pointing. Can you see and create similar shapes when drawing the dragons feet and hands? Erase the lines you don't need.

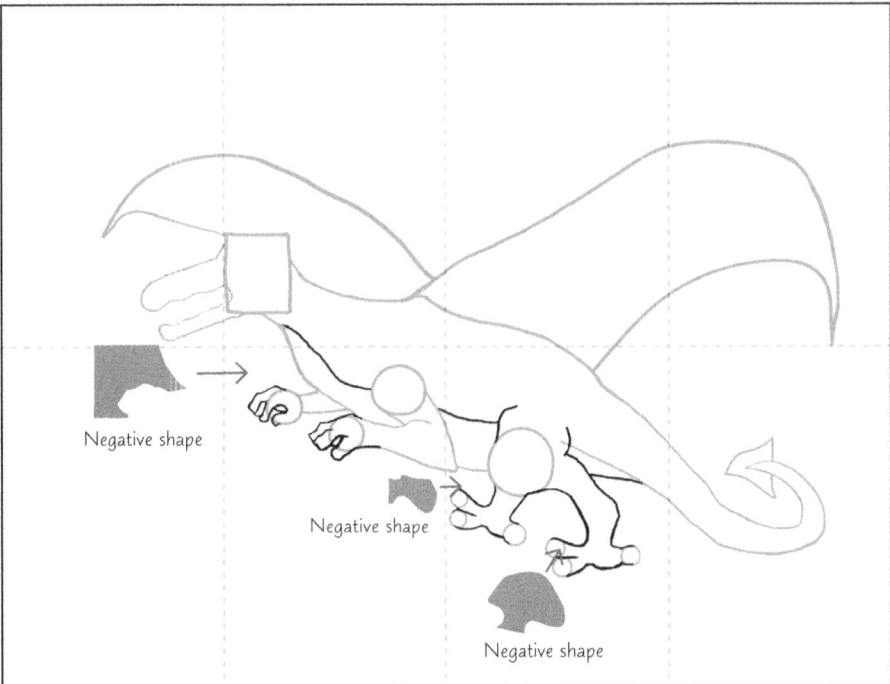

🌰 Step 6

Now boys and girls, let's draw some wavy and zig zag lines for the wings, hair, and teeth. Then draw the dragon's eye. It doesn't have to be exact. Also lets add the thick sharp claws and more curved lines for the belly. You are doing great!

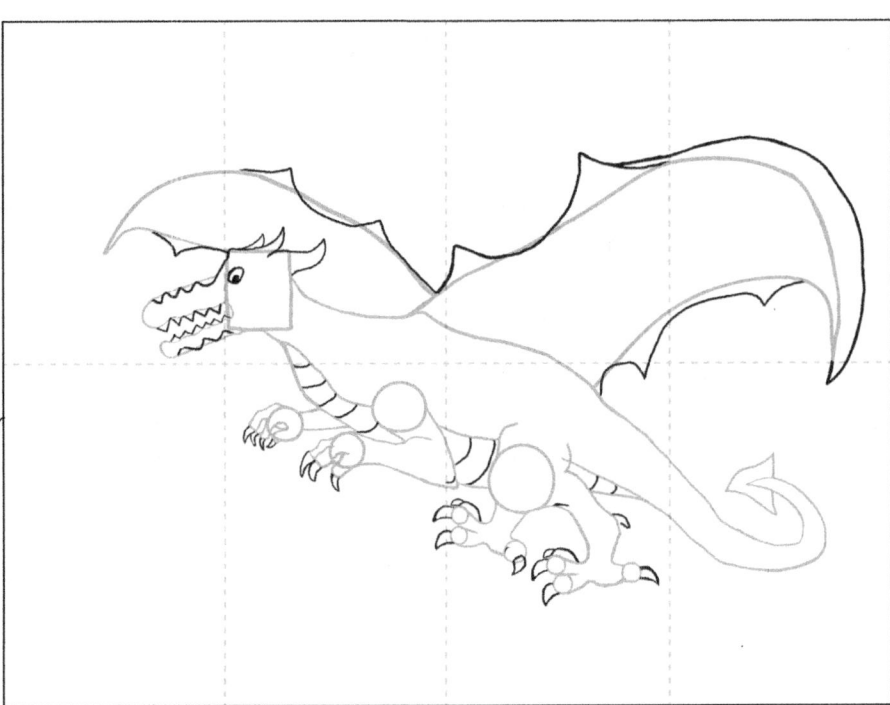

# Step 7

Add some more details to the dragon and the fire. To draw the fire it's like drawing waves and the letter "C" backwards. His back is like a shark's fin many times over.

Step 8

Finish by erasing extra lines. Touch up by making some lines thicker or darker.

The world and its desires pass away, but whoever does the will of God lives forever. For where your treasure is, there your heart will be also.

Learn to Draw: Sword in Stone

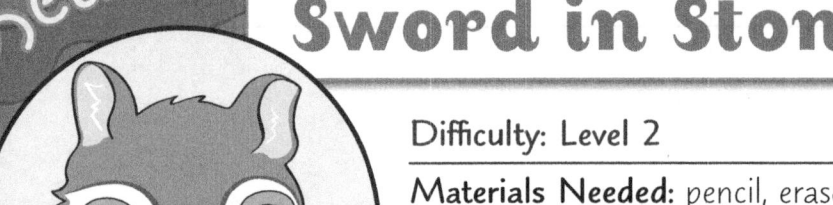

Difficulty: Level 2

Materials Needed: pencil, eraser, 8 1/2" x 11" paper.

The Sword in Stone is a long ago legend about King Author and the Excalibur. Only the rightful heir to the king could pull the sword from the stone.

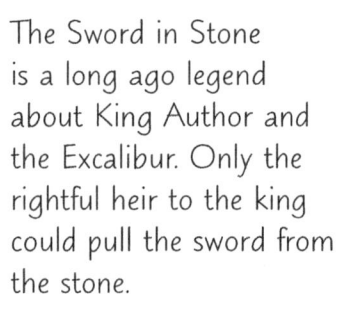

 Step 1

Let's look for some simple shapes in the Sword in Stone. The biggest shape I see is an oval for the stone (#1). A rectangle for sword's blade and handle (#2). A circle for the handle top. (#3).

 Step 2

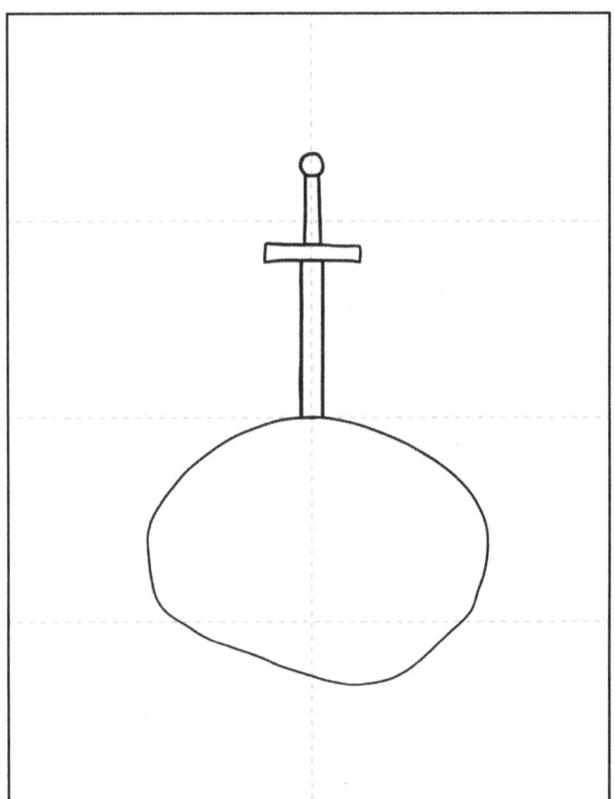

Take a blank sheet of 8 1/2" x 11" paper. Fold the paper in 8 sections as outlined on page 6 of this book. Draw an oval with the top in the center of the paper and the bottom below the third fold mark. Draw three rectangle shapes for the sword and a small circle near the top of your paper for part of the sword handle.

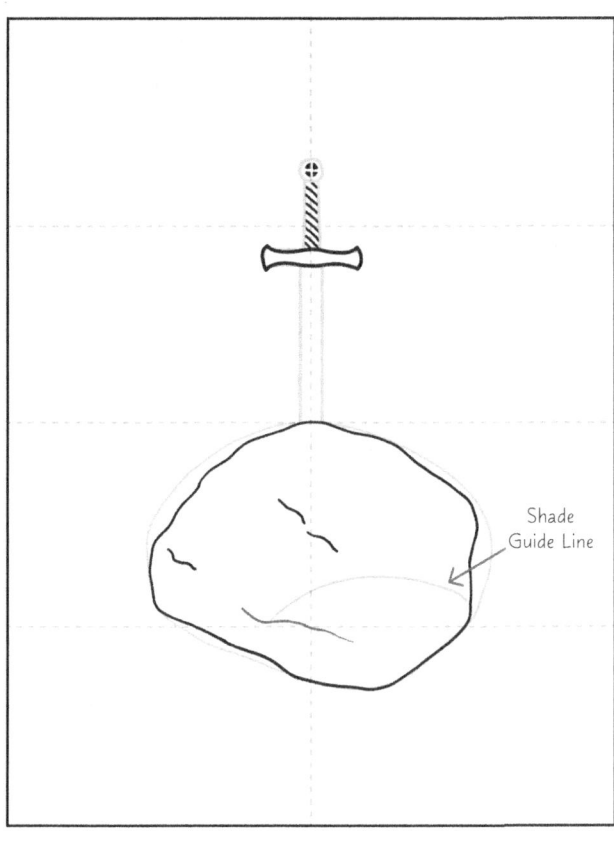

Shade Guide Line

Step 3

Define the rock with some bumpy lines and draw a light guideline to help with shading. Draw some symmetrical curved lines for the horizontal handle. Add a striped line pattern for the shaft of the handle and a cross decoration inside the circle.

Shading tip

One technique for shading is called cross hatching. I like to think of shading like coloring, but instead of using a crayon we are using a pencil. Lightly go back and forth without lifting your pencil to fill in an area, then lift your pencil and do it again in a different direction. Keep repeating in different directions until your shade looks smooth. This cross hatching technique will give you more of an even texture. You can also use it to darken in areas instead of making heavier strokes that may look uneven.

Step 4

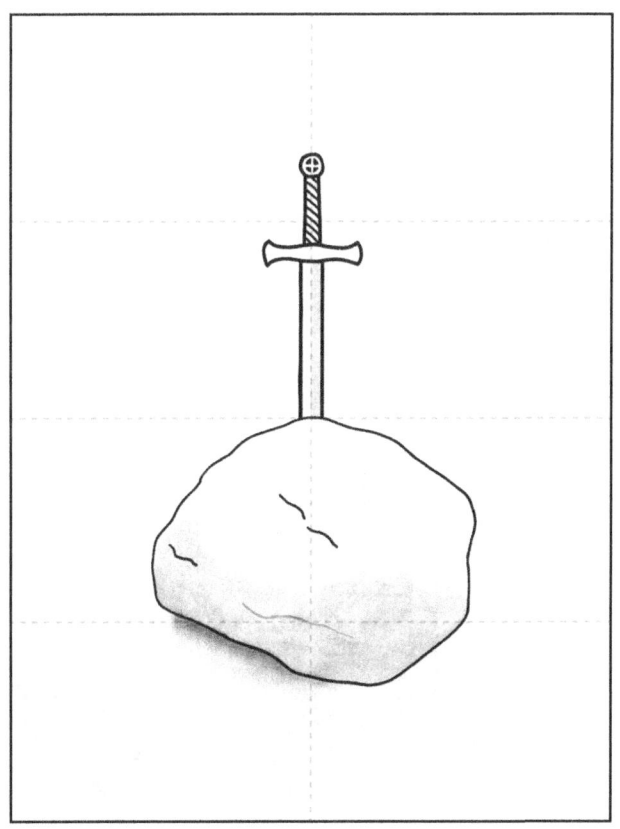

Now for some shading to make it look more real. First erase the lines you don't need. With the side of your pencil lightly go back and forth and fill in the bottom of the rock up to your guideline with light strokes. Make sure your guideline blends with the shading. If not erase it and start again. Don't get discouraged if it is not looking how you want it since shading takes a lot of practice. Shade on the left bottom outside of the rock too. This will make the rock look like it is resting on the ground. Finally add some light shading in the middle of the rock and on one half of the sword blade. Great!

Sword in Stone you come into my dreams and choose me to defend your kingdom.

Secrets of How to Draw Better
Yarn Hair Face Drawing

Difficulty: Level 3

Hey kids did you know that your eyes are in the center of your head! Don't believe me? Have your parents measure your eyes from the top of your head and then to your chin. You will find that the distance is the same. In this Activity we will draw a face with the right proportions and use yarn for hair

Materials Needed: pencil, eraser, scissors, yarn, glue, crayons or markers, 9" x 12" heavy white paper.

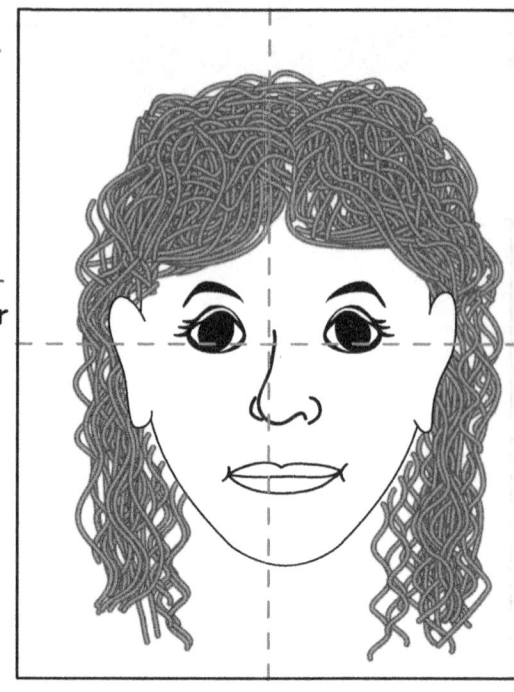

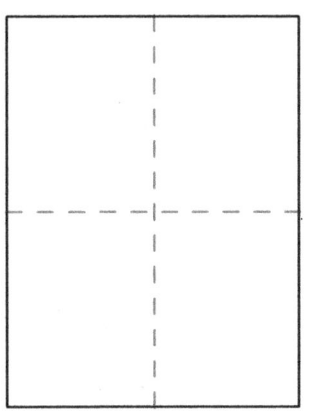

 **Step 1**

Fold paper in half both ways. Draw eyes on the horizontal center fold mark. Next draw a nose on the vertical fold mark, then draw the mouth below the nose. Look at peoples eyes, nose and mouths when they're mad, happy, sad, or just silent. In the back of the book on page 82, there are some examples of face parts to help you draw.

Step 2

Now you are going to draw the head. Heads are oval in shape some are long and some are fat. Look at the shape of peoples heads around you or in a picture to get an idea. To draw the head with the right proportions, first mark where you want the bottom of the chin. Next take a ruler and measure from the chin mark you just made to the center fold mark. Now use the same distance to measure from the fold mark to the top of the head and mark that with your pencil. Draw an oval from these two marks. If you are having trouble you can use the template in the back of the book

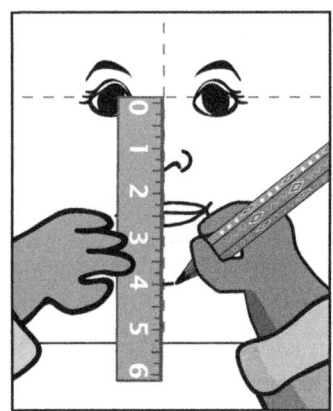 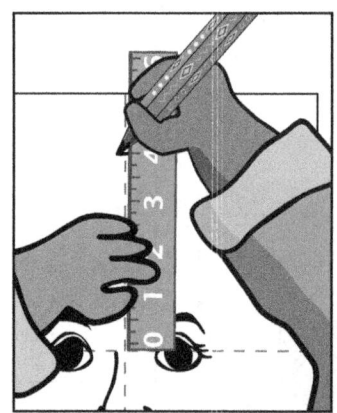 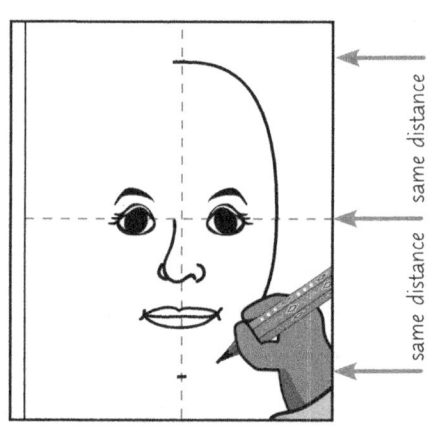

Step 3

Draw ears just above the fold mark on the outside of the oval. Draw the eyes on the horizontal center fold mark. Draw the nose and lips, lined up with the vertical center mark. See page 82 on ideas for drawing different eyes, noses and lips, along with other interesting features.

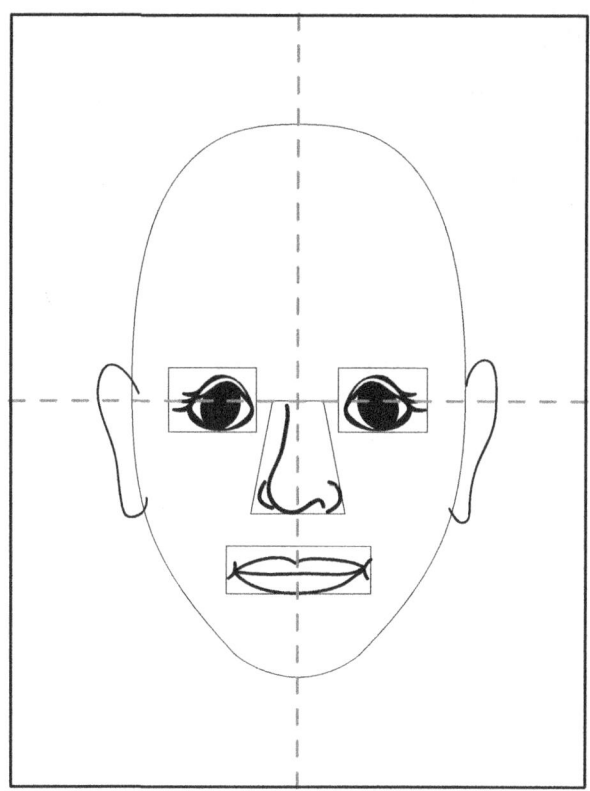

Step 4

Cut yarn in different sizes. You might want to cut short pieces for a boy with short hair, or longer pieces for a girl with long hair. Glue Yarn onto top portion of head. Don't forget to draw other details like eye lashes, eye brows, and maybe glasses, or earrings.

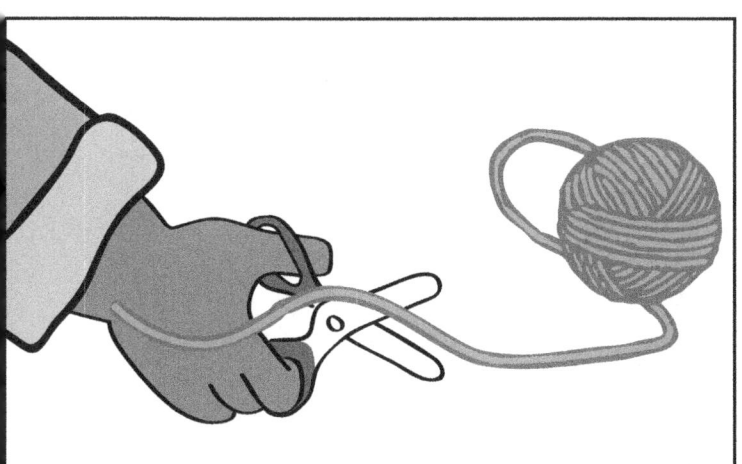
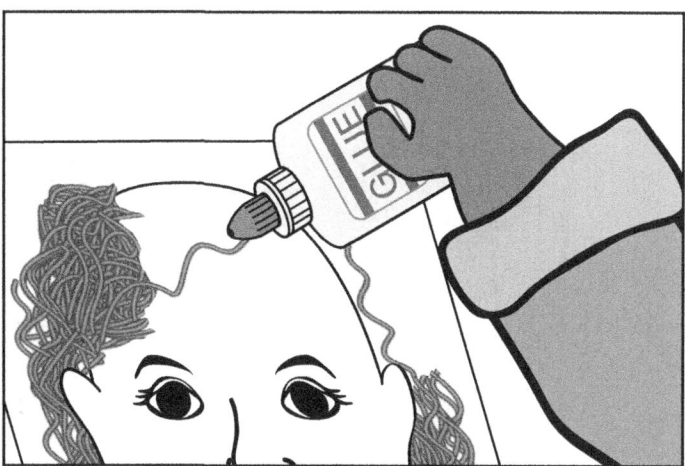

Parents: Most children and even adults put the eyes at the top of the head when drawing. The reason for this is that the face features are more interesting than the hair. Therefore, in our subconscious things we find interesting are made bigger while things less interesting come out smaller. By using yarn for hair it becomes more interesting again and our perception changes to include the top of the head as an important element. The reality of the eyes in the middle of the head even surprises adults. If you measure it out and children see that it is the same distance, it will greatly strengthen their face drawing skills.

Learn to Draw
Wizard

Difficulty: Level 3

Materials Needed: pencil, eraser, ruler, 8 1/2" x 11" paper.

Wizards were known to have magical powers. They were skilled at making magical potions and medicines out of mystical herbs. Good wizards would help the king sort out troubles and sometimes they used crystal balls to foretell the future.

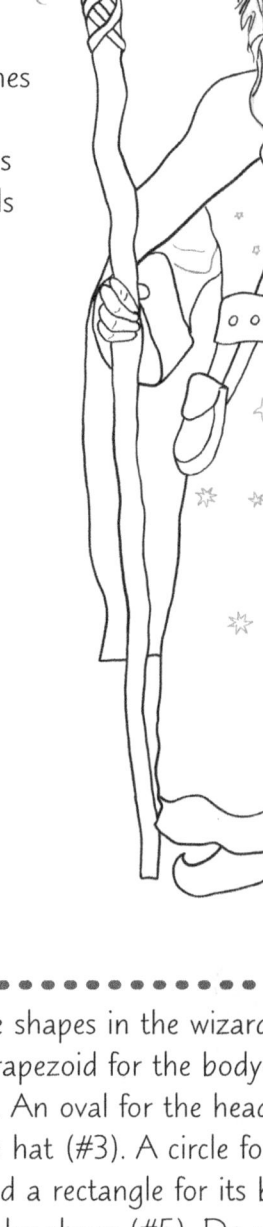

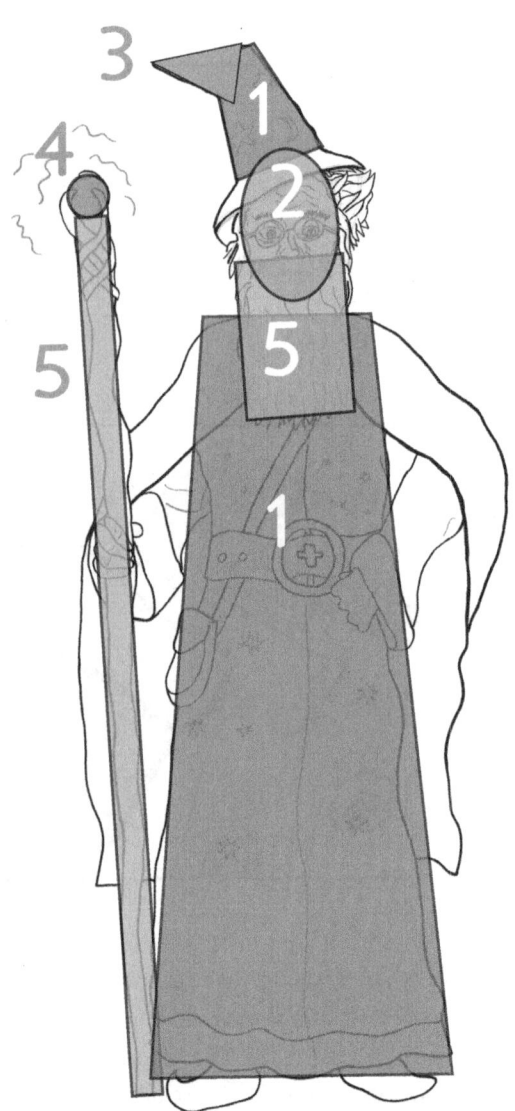

 **Step 1**

Let's look for some simple shapes in the wizard. The biggest shape I see is a trapezoid for the body and a small one for the hat(#1). An oval for the head (#2). A triangle for the top of the hat (#3). A circle for the top of the magical staff (#4), and a rectangle for its body. The beard also has a rectangular shape (#5). Do you see any more simple shapes? Awesome.

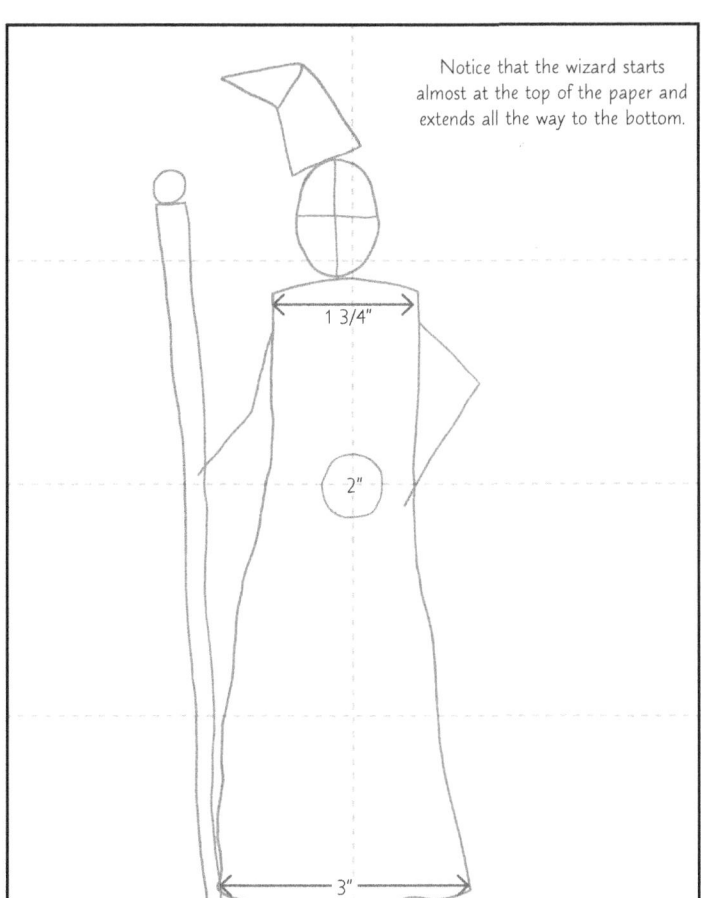

Notice that the wizard starts almost at the top of the paper and extends all the way to the bottom.

Step 2

Take a blank sheet of 8 1/2" x 11" paper. Fold the paper in 8 sections as outlined on page 6 of this book. Lightly draw all lines so we can erase them more easily later. Sometimes it's best just to take a ruler and measure. So let's do that. In the center of the paper draw a circle that is 2" x 2". Next draw the body with a rough measurement of 3" wide on the bottom and 1 3/4 " wide at the top. Now with these shapes drawn we can get an Idea of how big to draw the rest of our shapes by using the fold marks as guidelines. Make sure the staff is more narrow on the bottom. If you make a mistake, erase it.

Step 3

Let's continue by drawing the rim for the hat, a square shape for the beard and work on the wizard's cloak. Make sure to look carefully at where your fold marks are in relation to your drawing. Let's draw some shapes for the hands. One looks like a trapezoid.

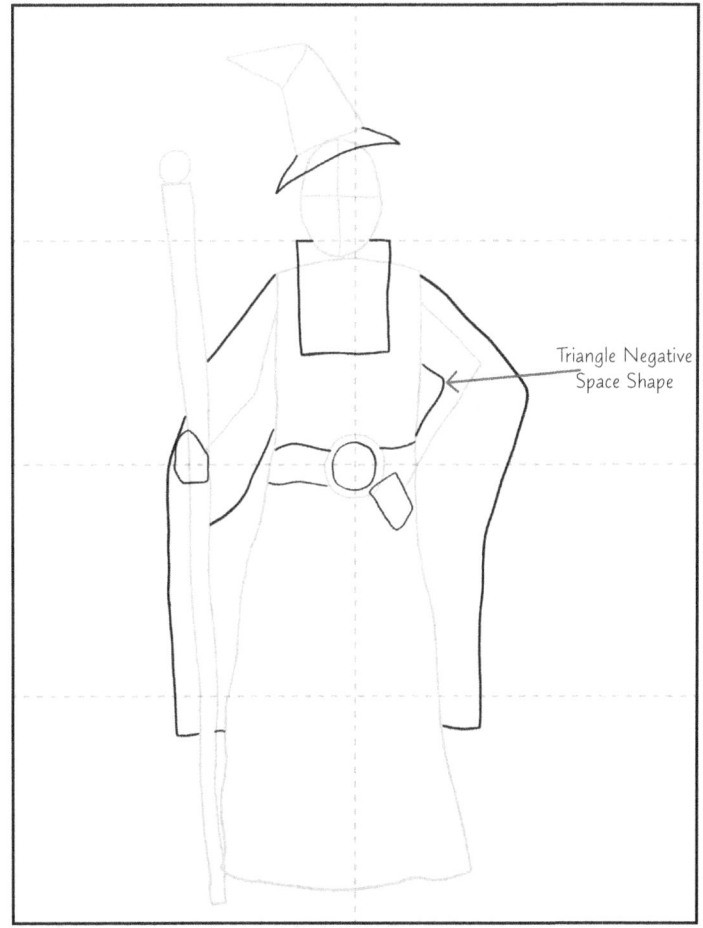

Triangle Negative Space Shape

Learn to Draw

Wizard continued

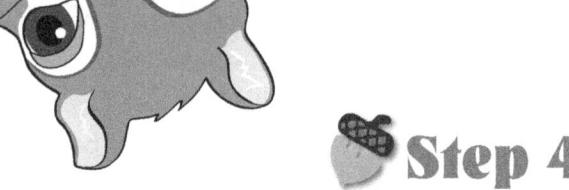

Step 4

Next outline the hat with a more expressive line. Add the eyes on the horizontal cross mark you drew earlier. Eyes are always in the center of your head. Draw the rest of the facial features including the hair and beard. Draw in more details for the wizard's staff with parallel curvy lines. That's coming along nicely.

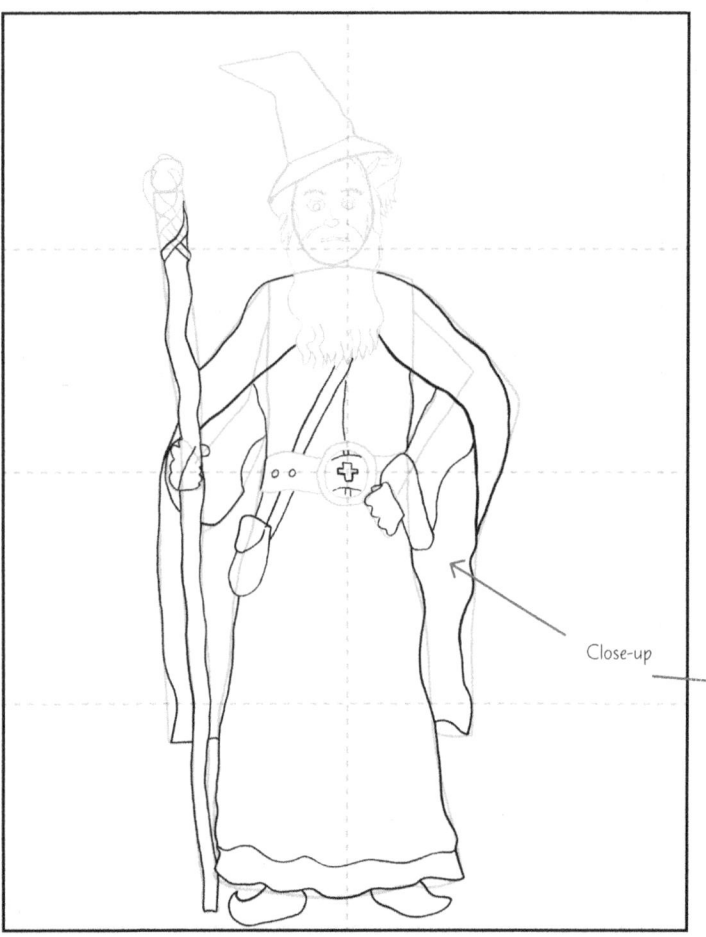

Close-up

Step 5

Erase the lines you don't need and add more details to the body. When I think of clothing, I think of flowing lines. Let's define his cloak with wavy curvy lines. Define the staff in the same manor by adding curved lines. Draw the wizard's pouch. When you are drawing, always compare the size of your shapes to each other. Notice that the hands are just a little smaller than the pouch. Speaking of hands let's define them more with curved lines that look like knuckles. On the left hand draw a diagonal line to use as a guide. Don't forget the feet!

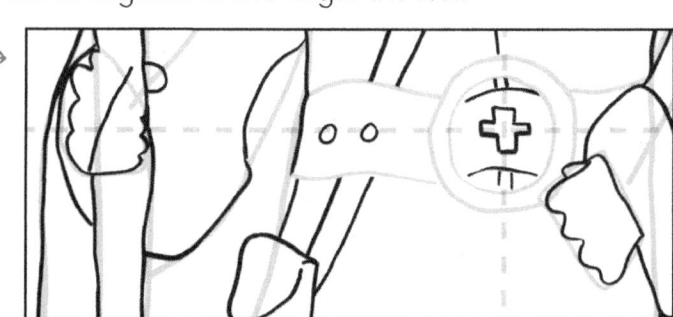

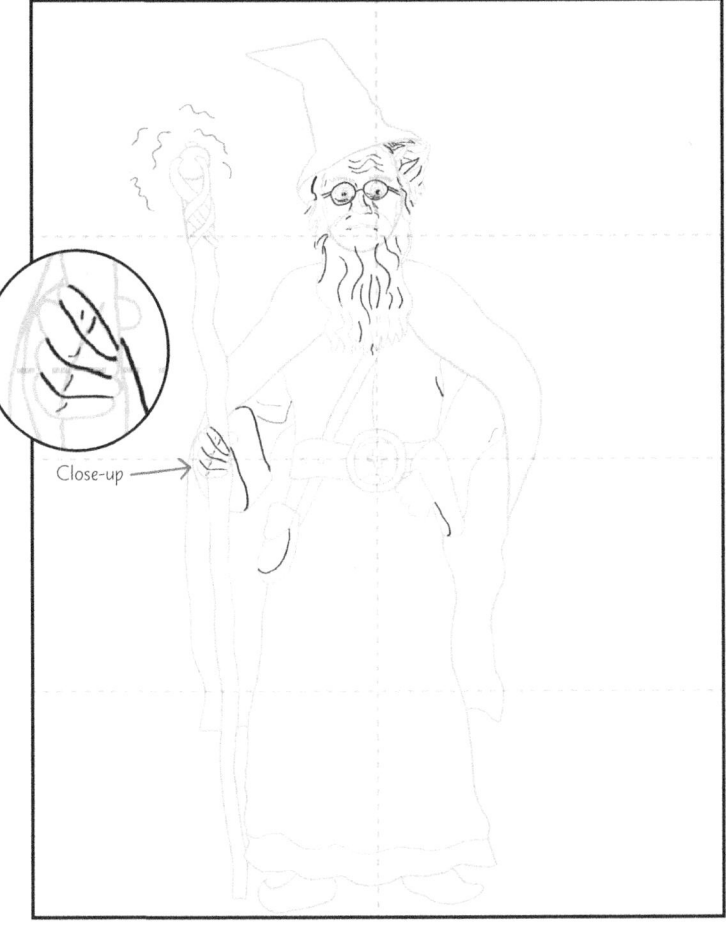

 **Step 6**

Continue to add details to your wizard. Give him some glasses and wrinkles to make him look old and wise. Finish his hair and beard with more wavy and curved lines. Fill in his eyes. Add light mysterious squiggle marks near the top of his staff. For the left hand, use the diagonal line you drew in the previous step to line up the knuckles to the fingers. That's nice.

Erase the lines you don't need

Step 7

By using the side of your pencil and moving it back and forth lightly, you can add some shadows to your drawing. Let's do that to the bottom of the hat, the staff orb and to some of the lines for the hair, beard and eyes. Lightly draw in the patterns of stars and moons for the hat and stars for the clothing.

 Finish by erasing extra lines. Touch up by making some lines thicker or darker.

Now your wizard is ready and wise to help out the king. When I was young I sought wisdom. For she is close to those who seek her, and the one who is in earnest finds her.

Secrets of How to Draw Better
Self Portrait

Difficulty: Level 3

Vincent van Gogh, a famous artist, painted himself many times. In this secret we discovery one way the great artist's learned how to draw, and that was to draw themselves.

Materials Needed: Mirror, pencil, eraser, white paper or drawing pad, drawing board, masking or artist tape.

Step 1

Place the mirror in front of you so you can see your face. Sit in front of the mirror and try to draw yourself. First start with an oval for your head. Next in the center of the oval, lightly draw two perpendicular lines. Perpendicular is a big word that means the lines cross each other.

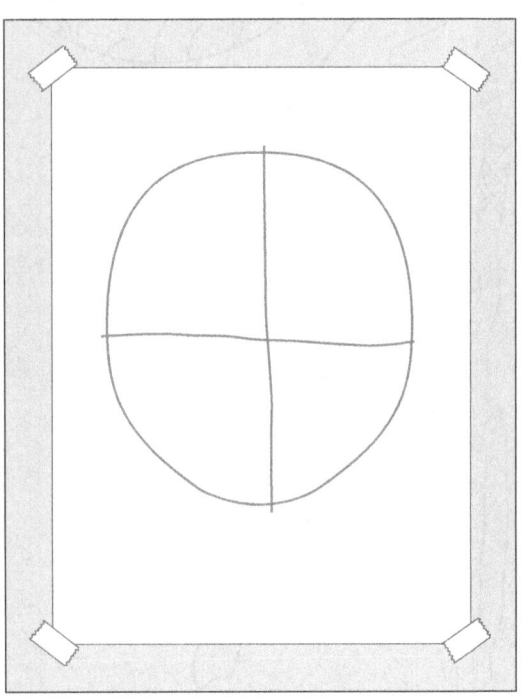

Step 2

Now start drawing your own face, remembering to put the eyes, nose and mouth on the perpendicular lines. Don't get discouraged if it doesn't look like you. It takes many years of practice to make perfect drawings like a professional artist's.

Parents: As kid's, the "self" is very important to them. Children are learning their own identities. By drawing ourselves we get in touch of who we are and how our face is proportioned. Also we don't need someone else to pose for us. Instead of drawing from a photograph, drawing from life is more challenging and fun.

Secrets of How to Draw Better

Stained Glass Tracing

Difficulty: Level 1

Tracing can be a lot of fun and will help you get a feel for drawing.

Materials Needed: Tracing paper, masking or artist tape, pencil, eraser, crayons.

Step 1

Pick one of your favorite pictures from a comic, magazine or book. To not ruin your book, lightly tape the tracing paper over the picture with just a few small pieces of masking or artist tape.

Step 2

After tracing the picture remove your tracing paper and color it in with crayon.

Step 3

With a black crayon darken the lines so it looks like a stained glass picture. Now you can hang it on your window and watch how the sun will light it up.

Learn to Draw
Jousting Knight

Difficulty: Level 4

Materials Needed: pencil, eraser, 9" x 12" paper.

Jousting competitions took place at medieval tournaments that gave knights the opportunity to display their skills in battle. Knights charged each other on horseback using a lance to try to knock the other knight off his horse. The horse and knight were decorated based on the knight's coat of arms; a special symbol that represented his family.

 **Step 1**

Boys and girls, let's look for some simple shapes in the knight on a horse. I see lots of shapes. An egg shape for the head (#1). A rectangle for the knight's body (#2). Coming in at number 3. An oval for the horse's body and head (#3). A triangle for the horse's neck (#4). Many circles for the horse's legs and a circle for the horse's nose (#5). Do you see any more simple shapes? Great.

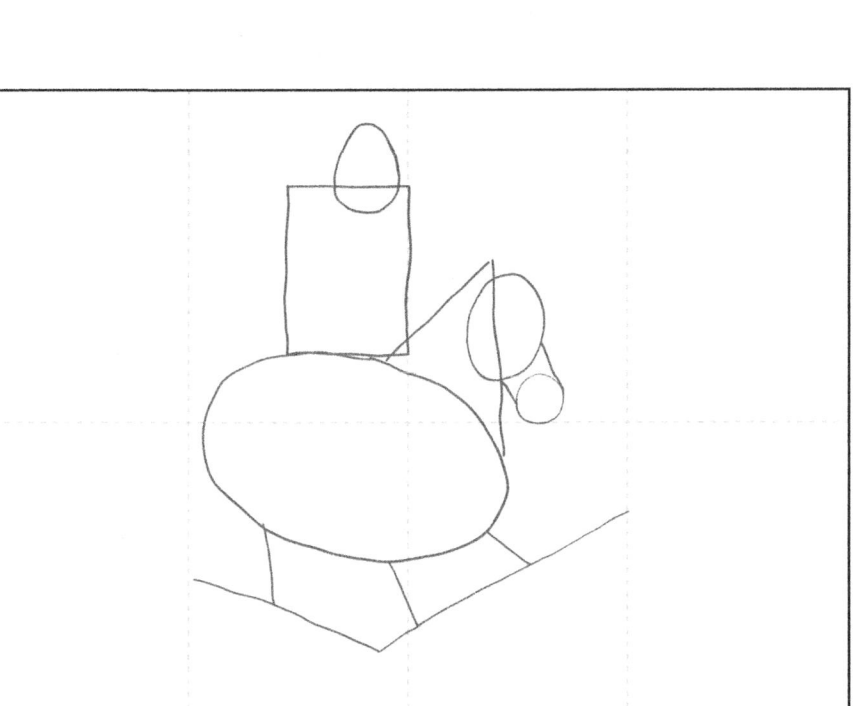

Step 2

Take a blank sheet of 9" x 12" paper. Fold the paper in 8 sections as outlined on page 6 of this book. Lightly draw an oval near the center fold marks. Notice that the oval is more to the left of the paper. Horses are difficult to draw so make sure all your shapes are in the right position. Compare negative shapes as well and use a ruler to measure if needed. Lightly draw in the rest of the shapes in relation to your fold marks. Lightly draw the bottom "V" like line that makes it look like a rocking horse. This is a guideline that you will use in the next steps.

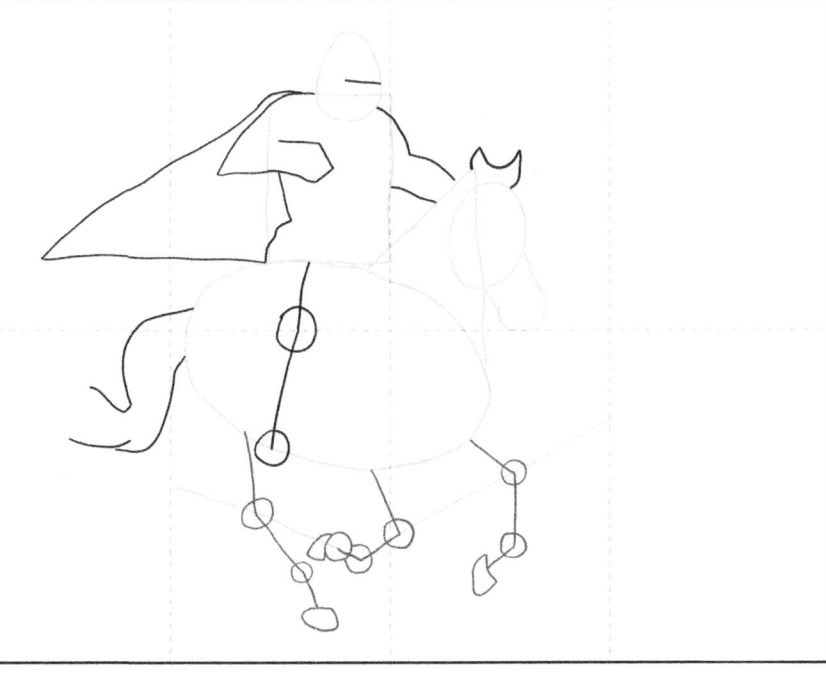

Step 3

Lets add some stick like lines for the legs and lightly draw in some circles where the line bends. These circles will help you connect lines for the thickness of the legs. Notice how we used that "V" line, to line up some of the circles. Draw in some lines for the tail, and a straight line for the knight's leg. Make sure to draw the circles on the night's leg in the right position. Draw a triangle for the cape, the knight's arms, more detail for the body and ears for the horse. All your lines should be still light at this point.

Learn to Draw
Jousting Knight continued

Step 4

Let's define some of the shapes and add more details. Draw the cape more wavy, add more lines to the tail, and more lines to the helmet. Draw in the fingers for the hand and make the lance with parallel lines. Draw the horses' and knight's legs by connecting the outsides of the circles. Wasn't that nifty? Finish the rest to the details.

Step 5

You are almost there. Erase some of the lines we don't need and let's continue with some more detail work. Draw diamond patterns for the horses front clothing. Draw in the horses' straps and add more detail to the horses' eye and nose. Let's not forget to draw in a stick line for the horses fourth leg, or else he will only have 3!

 Erase the lines you don't need

 **Step 6**

We are on the last leg (no pun intended) so let's finish that leg, then add some more details. The horse has a blanket with a pattern on its back end, so let's lightly draw in some criss cross lines. Textures and patterns sometimes look better when they are drawn lighter. The same thing goes for the tail. Let's draw some light curvy lines so the tail looks soft and bushy.

 Erase any more lines you don't need

 **Step 7**

This is the real last leg where you can erase any left over guide lines and darken in other lines.

Three things cannot long be hidden: the sun, the moon, and the truth.

Secrets of How to Draw Better

Grid Drawing

Difficulty: Level 2

A fun way to help you learn how to draw is to use a grid. By separating the picture into smaller squares, you will find it easier.

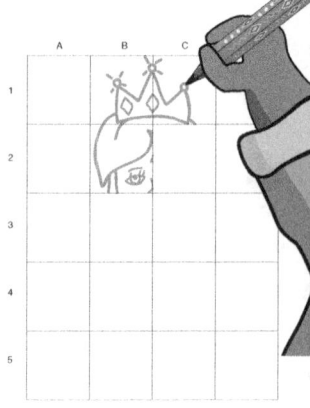

Grid Practice

First lets practice our grid skills. Use the numbers and letters on the drawing grid to find each section, then answer the questions. If you find it difficult, have your parents help you.

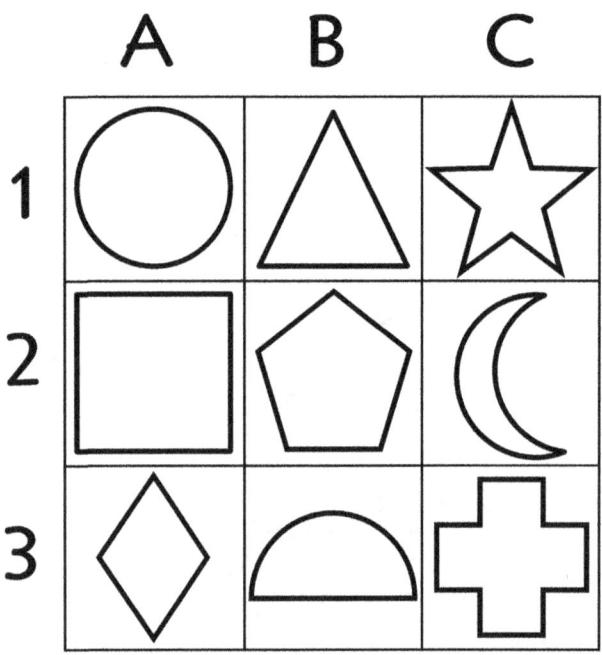

Questions

1). Circle the answer that shows what section the star shape is in?
   2C   1C   1B

2). Circle the answer that shows what section the circle shape in?
   2A   3B   1A

3). Circle the answer that shows what section the half moon is in?
   2C   3C   1B

4). Circle the answer that shows what section the cross is in?
   3A   3C   2C

5). Draw grid section 2A.

6). Draw grid section 3A.

Get more grids and a grid template in the back of the book.
Choose your own picture and place the template over it.

Complete the next few grid drawing activities on the next pages

Make Your Own Grid Puzzle

By placing a transparent grid onto a picture from a coloring book, magazine, calender, or book, you can make your own puzzle by drawing into each square.

Lay a transparency copy of grid A from the back of the book over a picture. Lightly tape down with small pieces of masking or artists tape. Make a photocopy of blank grid B also from the back of the book. Each square has a number and letter on it that matches grid A.

Pick a square to start. Draw what you see from that square onto the matching square. When you finished drawing each square you can color them in, and cut them out. Mix up the pieces and try matching them up again.

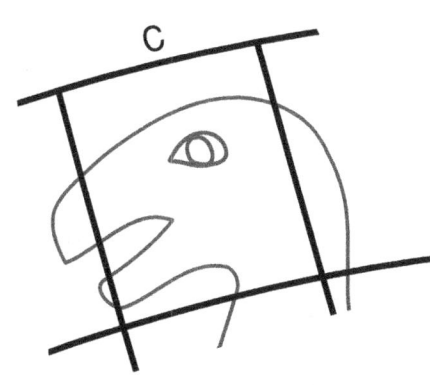

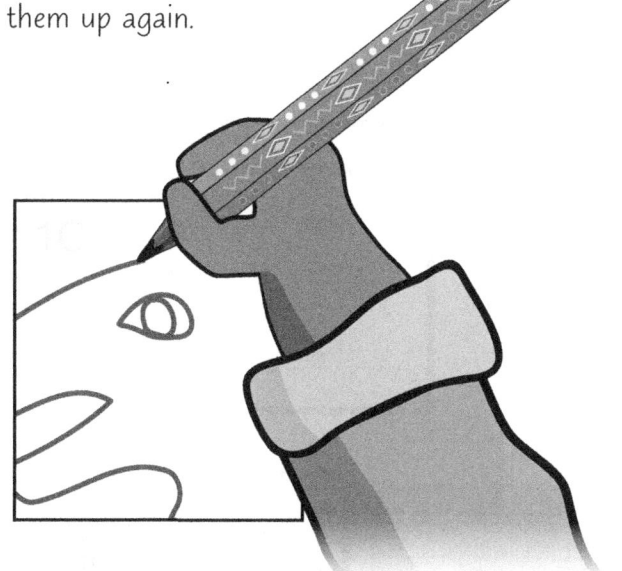

Parents: Grids help your child see relationship between what is called negative space (the space between objects or space that is not the subject matter) and positive space (the space that is the subject matter). When spaces are viewed as shapes, our ability to draw is greatly enhanced.

Drawing Grid Puzzle

Draw each square into its matching grid sections on the next page.

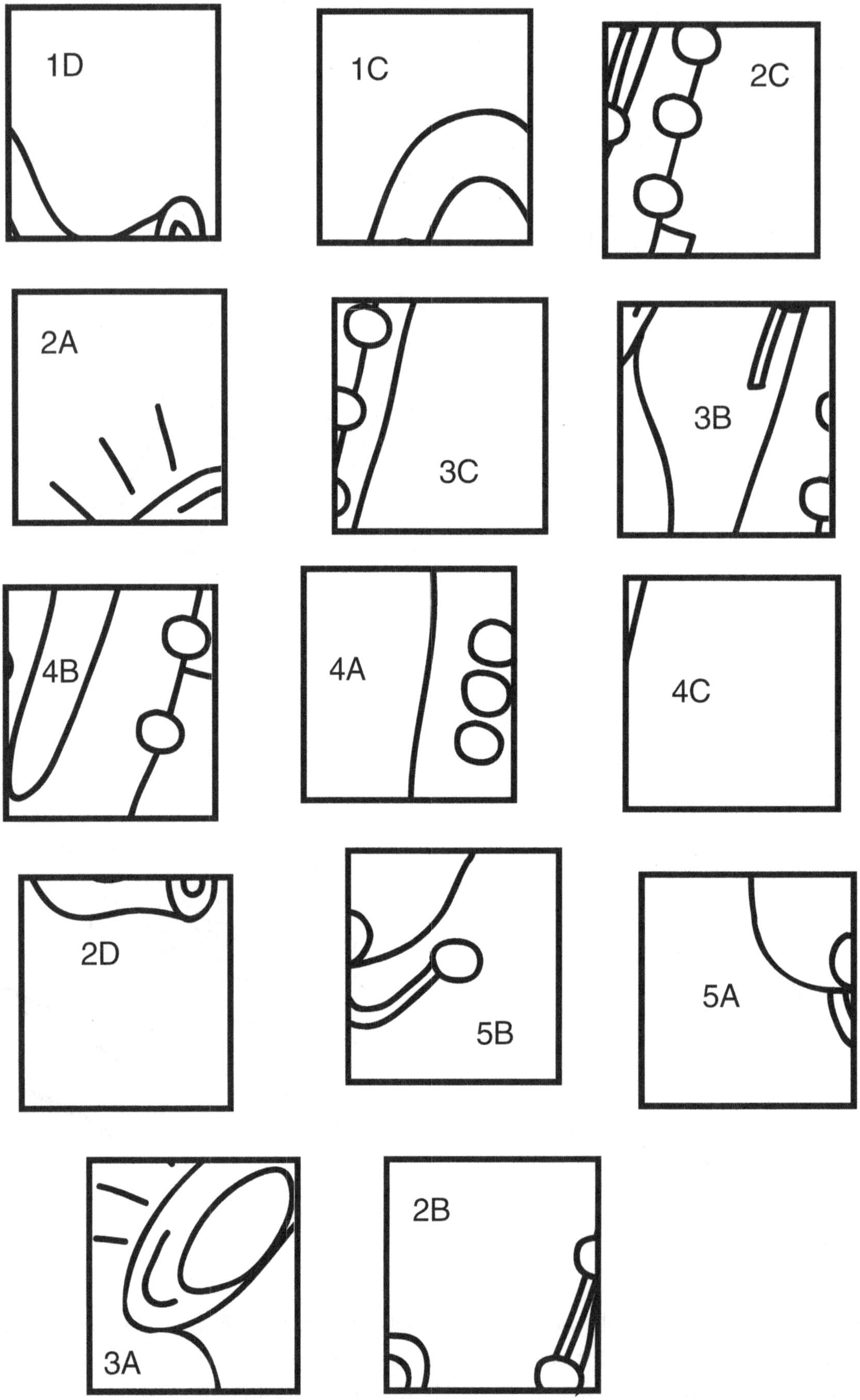

56

	A	B	C	D
1				
2				
3				
4				
5				

Make it bigger

Boys and girls, by using a grid you can make a drawing bigger. Match each section of the princess to the big grid on the next page to draw her. A helpful hint, when drawing in the squares, is to think of the objects shape, instead of what they are. For example if you are drawing an eye don't tell yourself it's an eye, but just look at its shape. Also look at the shapes around the object you're are drawing. This is called negative space.
By looking at both negative and positive space, you will draw better.

There are more Make it Bigger activities in the back of the book.

Don't be afraid to use your eraser boys and girls, if you make a mistake. Remember the eraser is your friend, and he likes it when he is needed. Most professional artists use erasers all the time. The eraser is their best friend.

	A	B	C	D
1				
2				
3				
4				
5				

Learn to Draw
Ogre

Difficulty: Level 2

Materials Needed: 9 x 12 sketch pad or paper, pencil, eraser.

The ogre is usually portrayed as a big dumb brute who is scary and has little to no feelings for others. A sort of ugly giant who may eat people; However, there may be good ogres like this fellow, who are perhaps just misunderstood, try to do good and don't eat people.

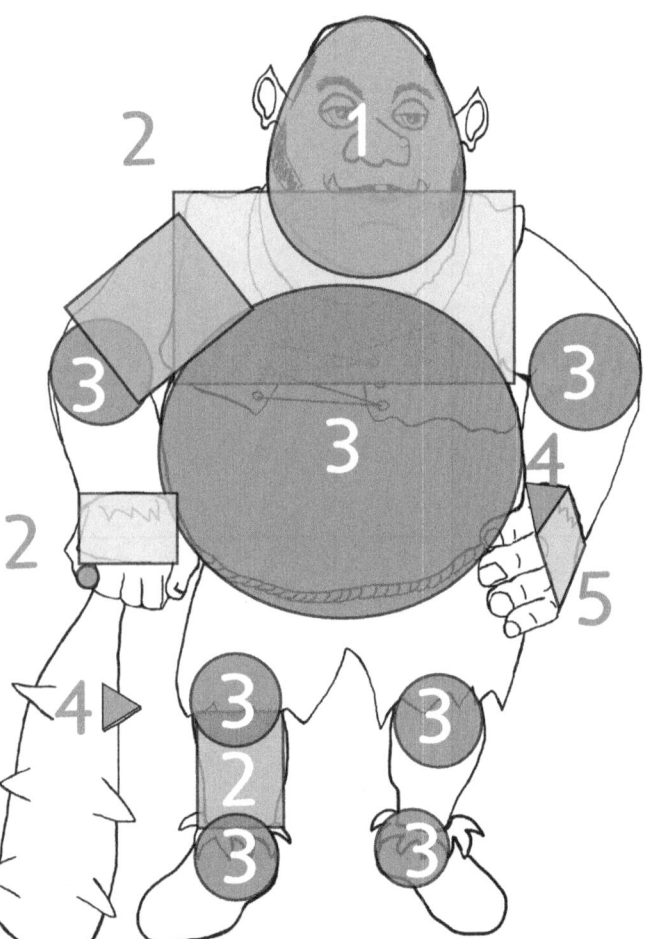

Step 1

Let's look for simple shapes. I see an oval or it's more like an egg shape for the ogre's head (#1). Squares and rectangles (#2). Circle for the belly and even though, I don't really see circles for the elbows and knee joints, I like to use them as a way to draw the arms and legs (#3). The spikes on the club a definitely triangles (#4). For the feet, let's put in some circle shapes (#5).

 **Step 2**

Take a blank sheet of 9" x 12" paper. Fold the paper in 8 sections as outlined on page 6 of this book. Look carefully at where your fold marks are in relation to the simple shapes. We will use these simple shapes as guides so draw lightly. Let's start with the big circle for the body. It is positioned towards the center of the page. Next a rectangle for the shoulders. It crosses the top fold mark. Draw the head, an egg shape, towards the top of the paper. Pay close attention to where it is positioned in relation to the vertical fold mark. It is more to the right of the vertical center fold mark. Draw the guides for the arms and legs and the stick lines that are in the center of each shape.

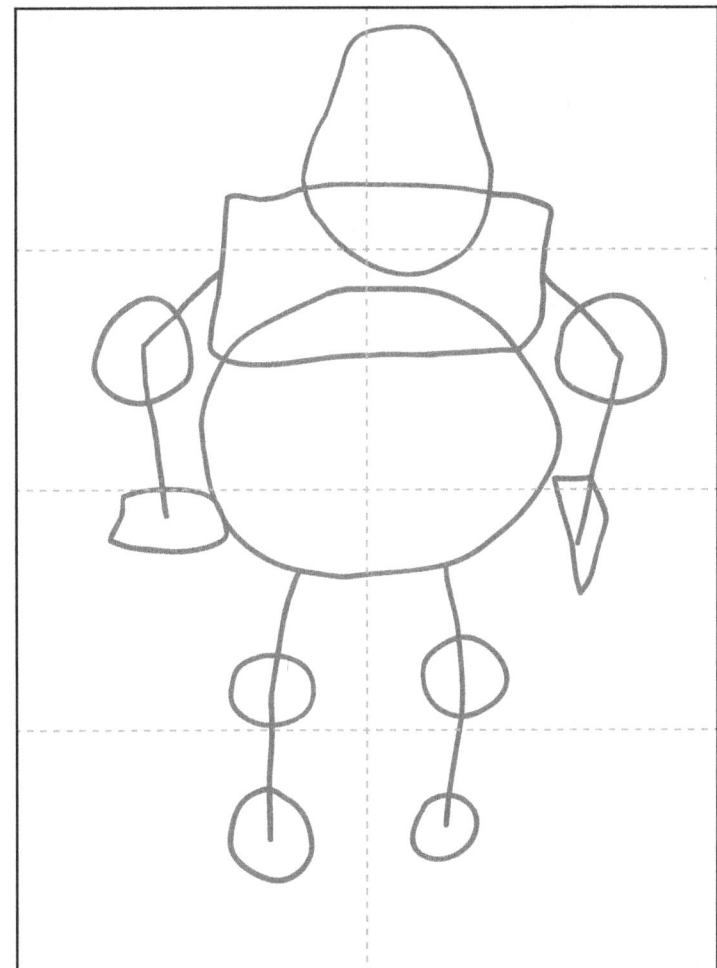

 **Step 3**

Let's draw the face. Since, we want his face to be goofy looking we are going to break the rules and draw his eyes closer to the top of the head instead of in the center. Lets first draw cross marks on the head so we can line up the eyes, nose and mouth. Next draw the eyes, nose and mouth. Don't forget the ears. Those are kind of like big tear drops or football shapes. Awesome.

Learn to Draw
Ogre continued

 **Step 4**

Let's draw the body, arms, legs and feet. I think of an ogre as being very bulky and strong with thick arms and legs. Use zig zag lines for the shorts. Make sure to look at your negative shapes, as well, to see if items line up.

 Erase the lines you don't need

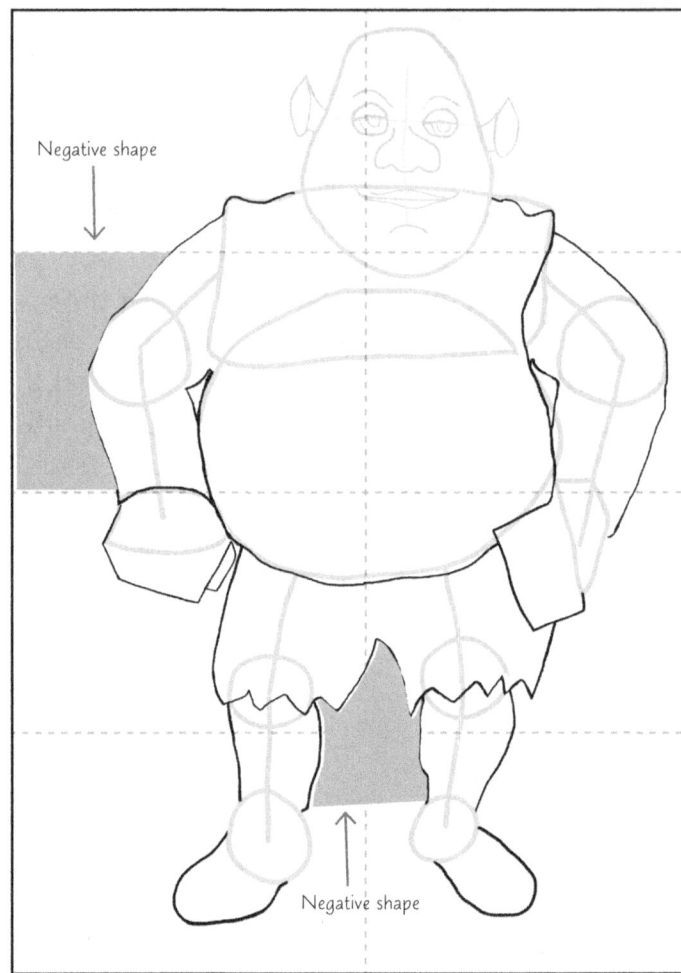

Negative shape

Negative shape

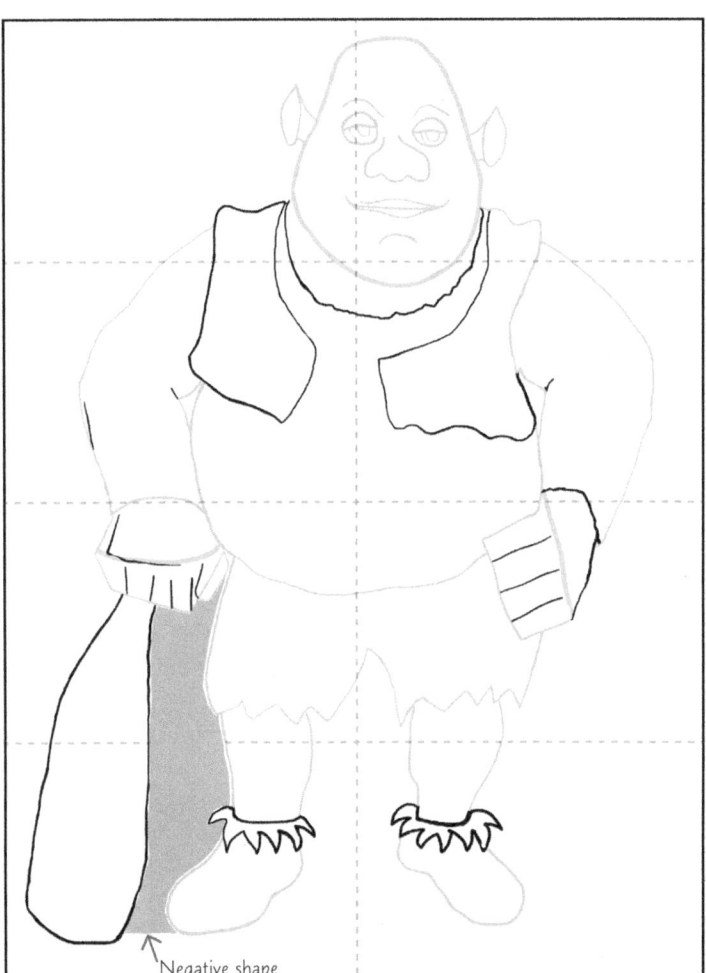

Negative shape

Step 5

Let's continue by drawing his vest and finishing the rest of his shirt. Draw lines for the fingers. Draw his big club and more zig zags for the top of his moccasins. Your doing great.

Step 6

Let's finish his face. For the eyebrows I used squiggly lines. Darken in all the areas that need to be dark. Remember your the artist. If you want to change something, go ahead. Perhaps you don't want the wort on his nose, different teeth or more hair on his head. Let's finish the hands by defining his fingers with some curved lines and more detail. Finish all other details like triangular spikes and the ties on his vest. Cool.

Start here for the rope belt by drawing one curved line then keep adding another. 1 2 3 etc...

Step 7

With an eraser remove any unnecessary lines. Darken and thicken any light lines where needed. Now your ogre is ready for action, like breaking in to that castle you drew earlier!

The hardest thing of all is to find a black cat in a dark room, especially if there is no cat.

Learn to Draw
King

Difficulty: Level 2

Materials Needed: 8 1/2" x 11" sketch pad or paper, pencil, eraser.

The King from medieval times, lives in a castle and rules over large areas of land and people known as his kingdom. To become the king, the oldest son of the king was next in line. The king had an army of knights to protect the kingdom from invasion. Even though he rules with absolute power, a good king is noble, just and merciful.

 **Step 1**

Let's look for simple shapes. I see another egg shape. The king's head is an upside down egg (#1). Trapezoids for the fur robe (#2). An upside down tear drop or a half circle and triangle shape for the robes pattern (#3). Circle, hexagon and diamond shapes for the crown. (#4, #5, #6).

Step 2

Take a blank sheet of 8 1/2" x 11" paper. Fold the paper in 8 sections as outlined on page 6 of this book. Starting from the topmost fold mark draw an upside down egg shape to the next fold mark. Make sure you draw the head more to the left of the vertical center fold mark. Next draw some cross guide marks for the eyes and nose. Notice how the horizontal guide mark is toward the middle of the head. Draw in the rest of the shapes paying close attention to the fold marks.

Step 3

Let's draw the face starting with the eyes. Football shapes with a circle in them that go on the guide lines you drew earlier. The nose and lips are centered with the guide lines. Draw the hair and crown with curved lines. For the top of the crown follow the shape we drew earlier with a wavy line. Draw some vertical straight lines on the points of the crown. This will help you in the next step. Develop the fur tunic with more curved defined lines and make those lines darker. Terrific.

Learn to Draw

King continued

Step 4

Let's develop the details of the face. Finish the beard with curved lines and give the king some wrinkle marks. For the crown draw parallel lines on the top following the previous wavy lines and use the guide marks we made to draw the crown's decorations. Lightly shade the eyeballs, some of the beard, face and tunic. Don't forget those cool looking eyebrows

 Erase the lines you don't need

Step 5

Now for the final touches. Draw in the jewels of the crown along the guide line, then erase the guide line. Draw upside down teardrops for the fur tunic pattern.

Step 6

Erase any lines you don't need and darken or thicken any lines that are too light. Your noble looking king is ready to rule his kingdom.

Wherever you go, go with all your heart.

Secrets of How to Draw Better
Chappy's Flash Card Shapes

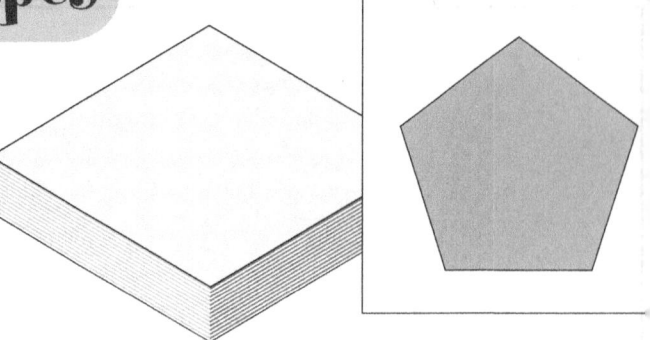

Difficulty: Level 2

Boys and Girls can you draw simple shapes from memory. Well, heres a great little game that will help you gain memory for drawing simple shapes.

Materials Needed: Thin cardboard, oak tag or 3 x 5 index cards, glue, shapes from book, paper, pencil, eraser.

 ### Step 1

On the next page and in the back of the book you will find the simple shape cards that you can cut out. If you want to make them firmer, like real cards, glue the whole page to some thin cardboard or oak tag, then cut them out.

Step 2

To play the game lay the cards face down in a stack and have your friend or parent flip the top card over to show you the shape for less than a second, then put it back face down again. Draw the shape you saw. When you are finished look at the card again to see how you did. Take turns at drawing and see how many shapes you got right. Don't worry if the shapes you draw are not perfect. As long as they match, you're a winner.

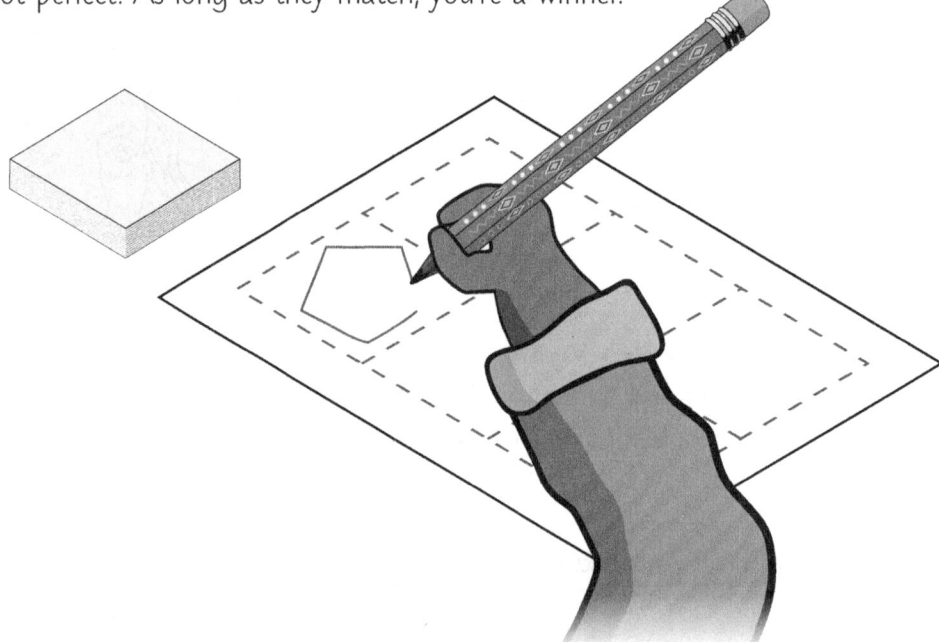

Parents: This will increase your child's memory for simple visual shapes. You can also print flash cards out onto card stock by visiting my website at www.chappythechipmonk.com/templates

Chappy's Flash Card Shapes

Bonus challenge: complex shape   Bonus challenge: complex shape

Also available online at: www.chappythechipmonk.com/templates

BACK OF FLASH CARD SHAPES PAGE

Secrets of How to Draw Better
Flip Chip Book

Difficulty: Level 2

Ever wonder how a cartoon is made. Well boys and girls, here's a fun project that will help us understand how an animation works. It will also increase our understanding of size and the position of an object.

Materials Needed: 3" x 3" or 3" x 5" post-its, pencil, eraser, black marker optional

Step 1

Let's Begin. First take your post-it pad and pull it apart so you have about 20 pages still bound. Draw a simple object on the last page in the pad, I have some examples listed. Draw lightly at first so you can erase more easily in case you make a mistake, then press down hard to outline your image before you go on to the next step.

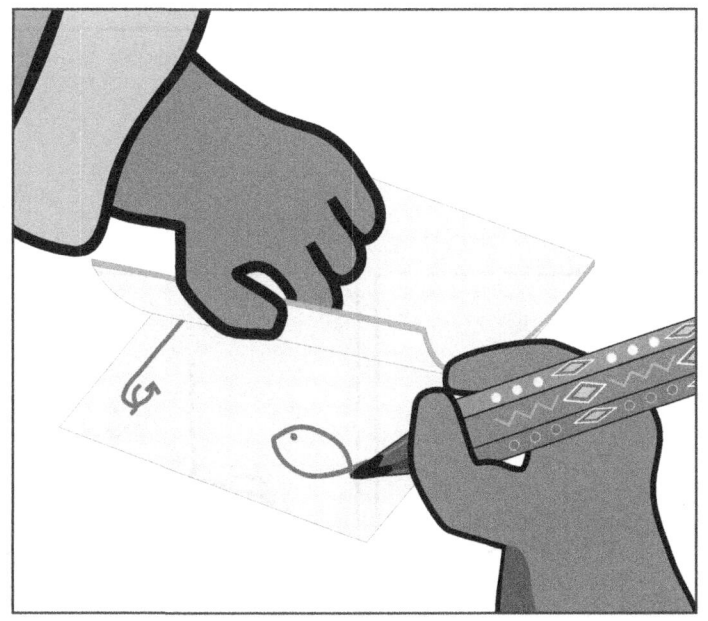

Step 2

Flip down the next page so you can see the first drawing underneath. Now Redraw your image almost exactly the same but slightly change its size, position, or shape. Repeat this step on every page, until you are finished. After finishing, use your thumb to quickly flip through your pages and see your drawings come to life.

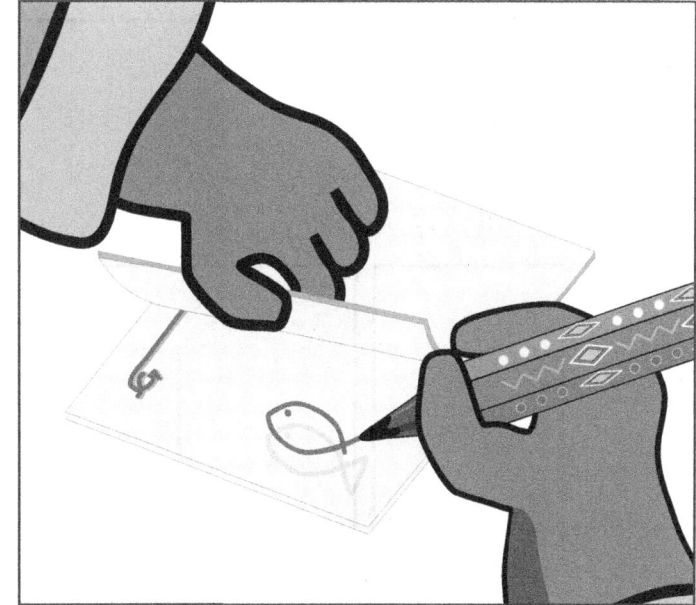

Parents: Shapes getting bigger, smaller and moving, will teach children the importance of size and position.

Flip Chip Book Examples

FLOWER GROWING

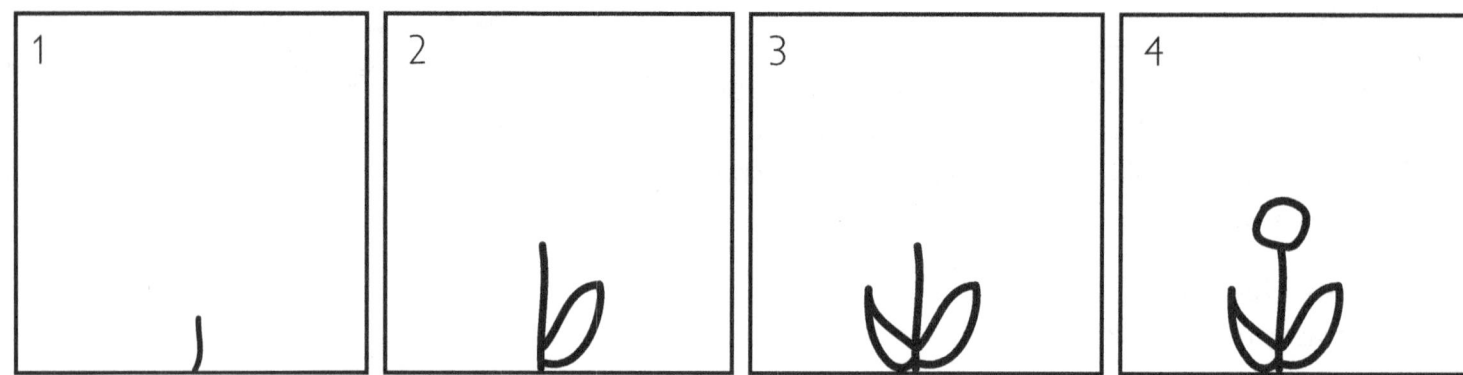

ARROW MOVING TOWARDS A TARGET

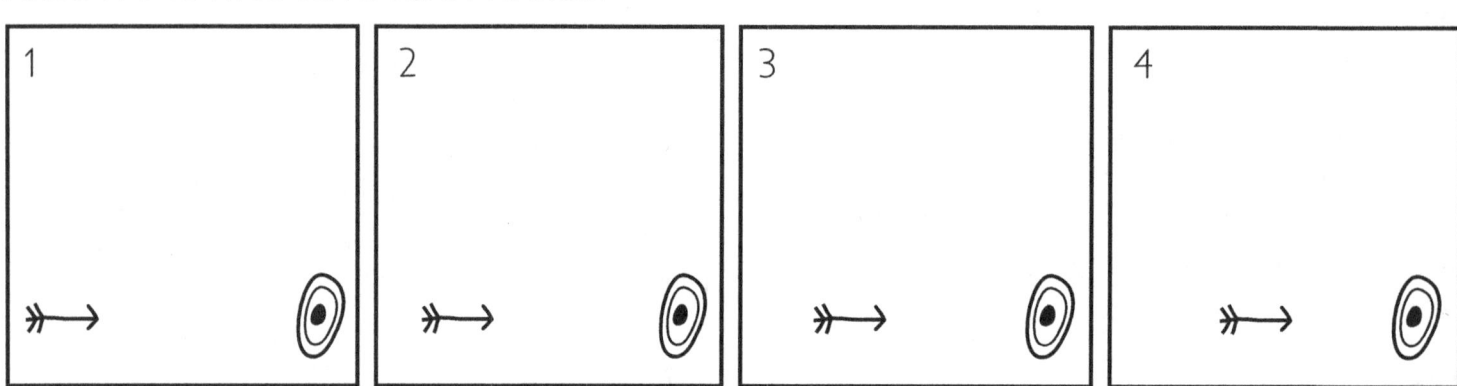

SPIDER MOVING UP A LINE

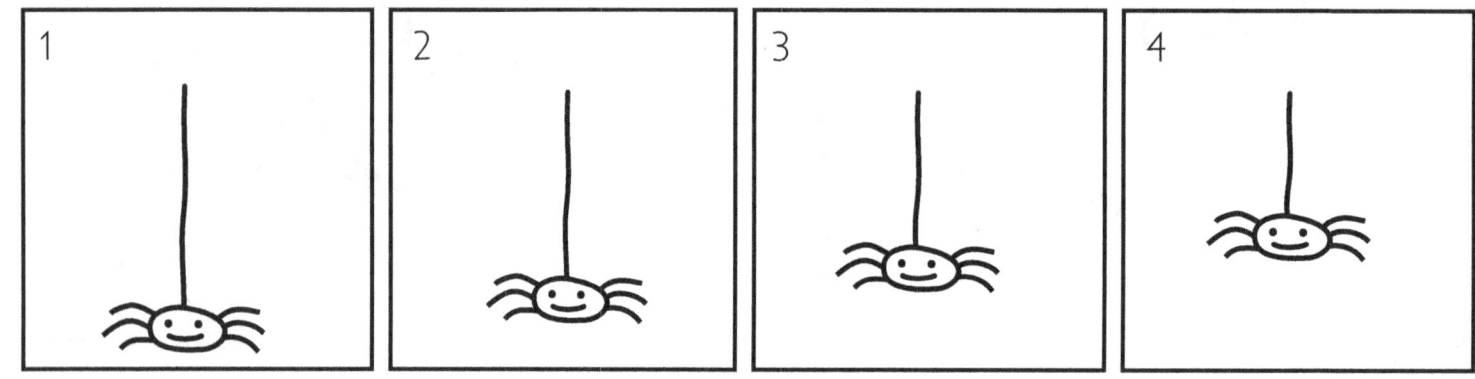

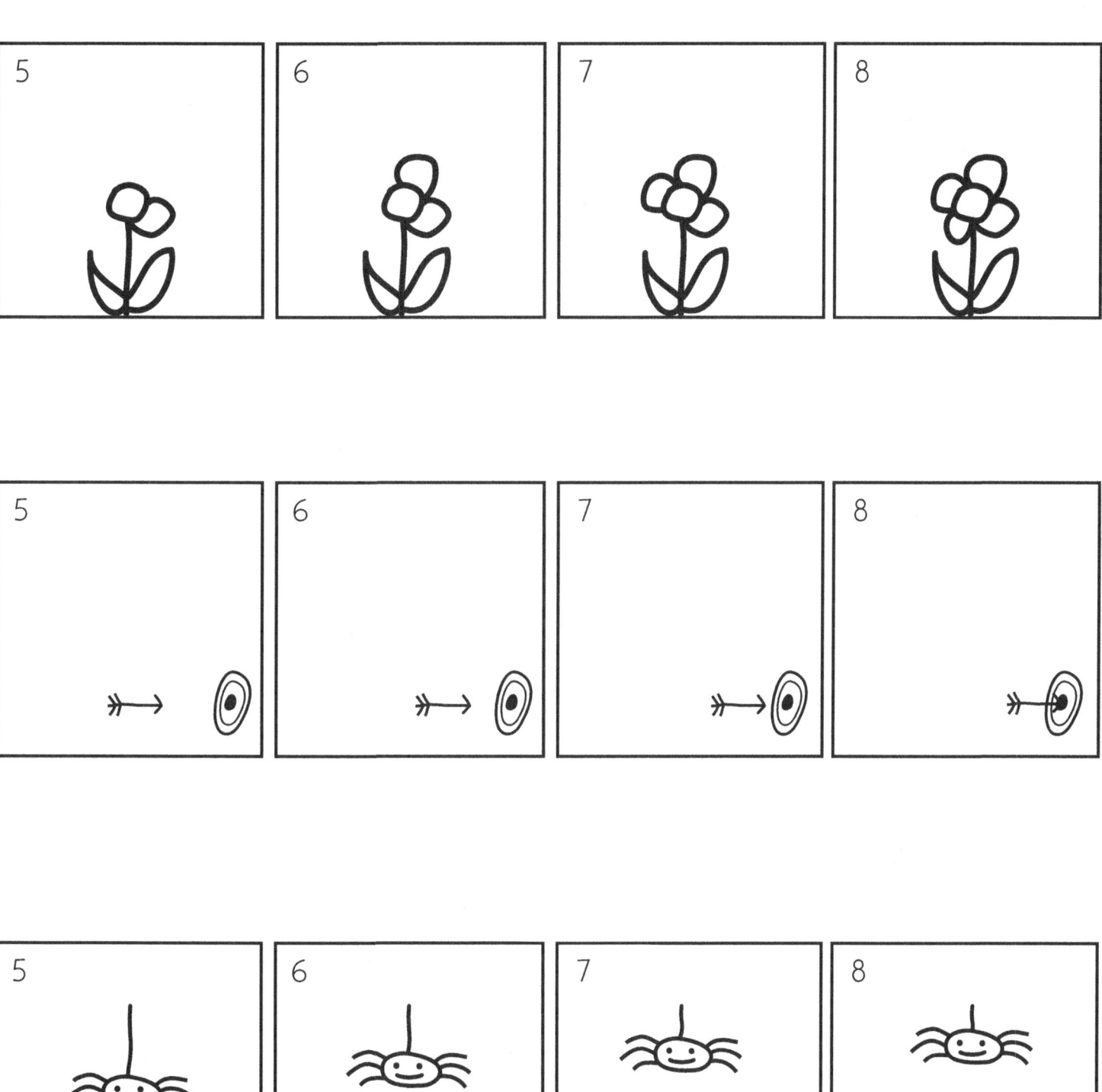

Flip Chip Book Examples continued

BUTTERFLY FLAPPING WINGS

 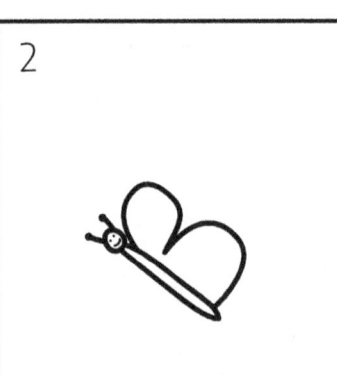 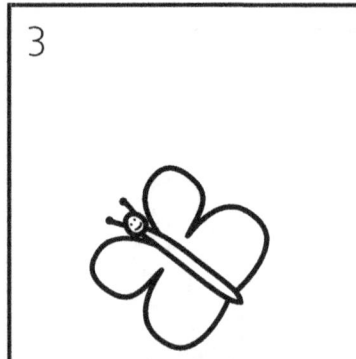 

FISH GETTING HOOKED ON A WORM

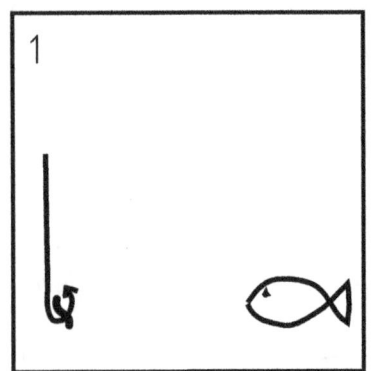 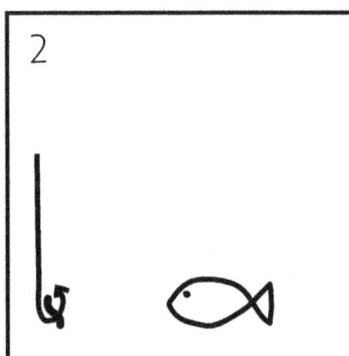 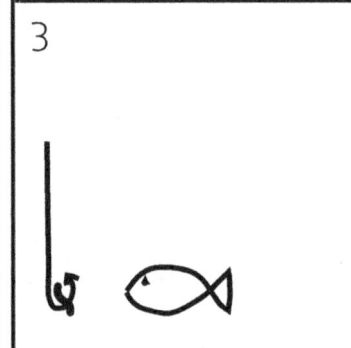 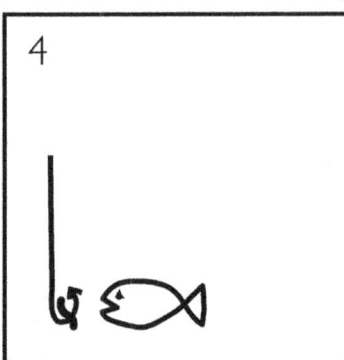

A BALLOON FLOATING UP

  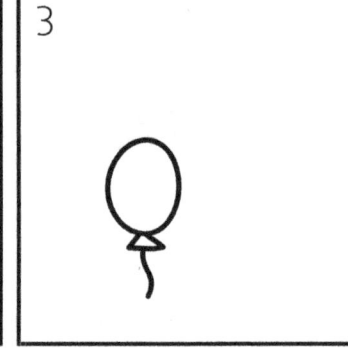 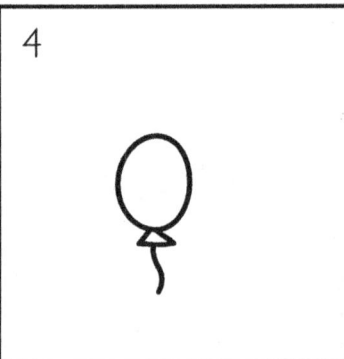

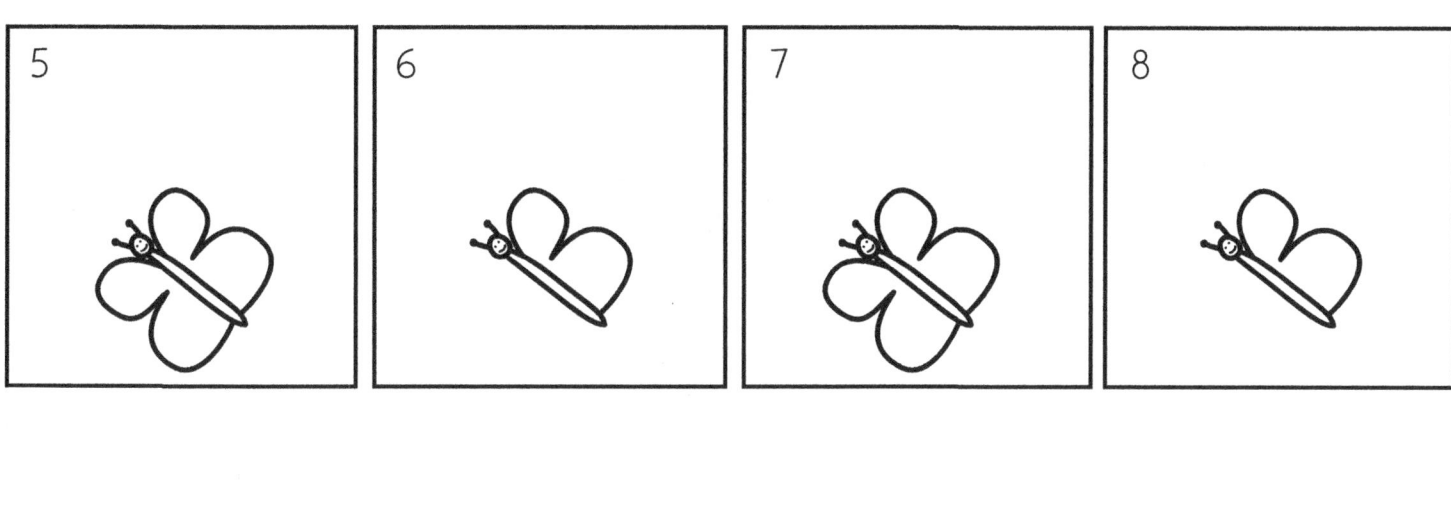

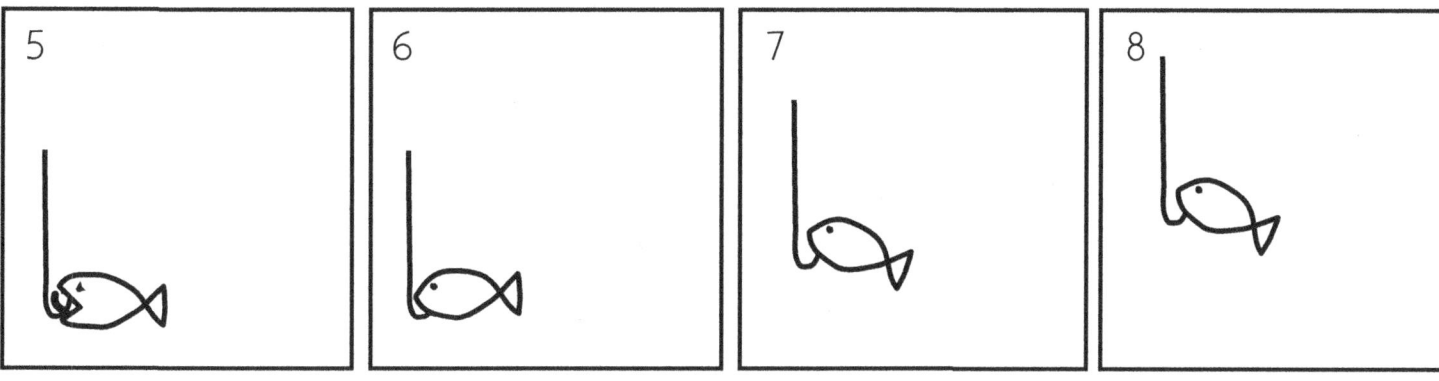

OTHER FLIP CHIP BOOK IDEAS:
One simple shape like a circle getting bigger, Bouncing ball, Fish eating another fish, Bowling ball knocking pins down

Chappy's

Extra activities and templates

Instructions: Best to photocopy template in case you make a mistake measuring. Paste template on back of, and in the center of an 11" x 14" or 9" x 12" black matte board or cardboard. Cut out shape.

Learn to Draw
Simple Shapes

Practice drawing simple shapes.
Trace on the dotted lines

CIRCLE   TRIANGLE   SQUARE

Using the space below, practice drawing the shapes

PENTAGON   HEXAGON   OCTAGON

Learn to Draw
Simple Shapes

Practice drawing simple shapes.
Trace on the dotted lines

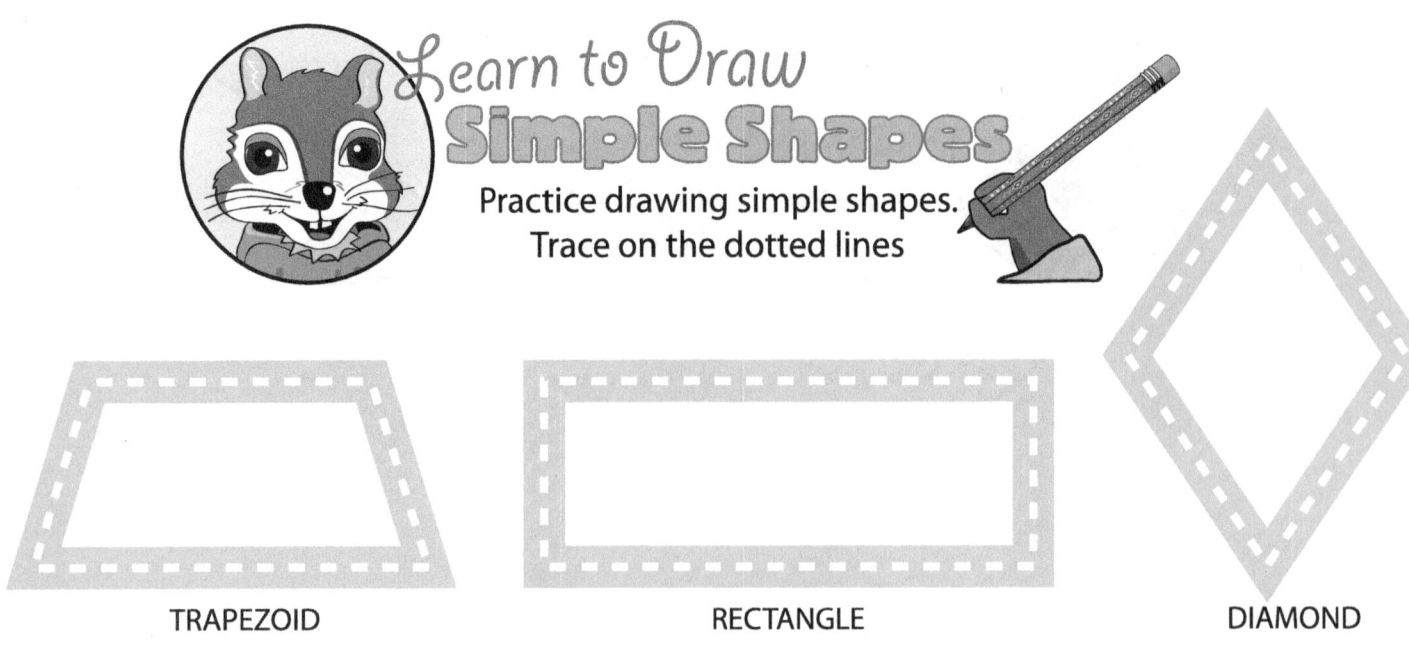

TRAPEZOID   RECTANGLE   DIAMOND

Using the space below, practice drawing the shapes

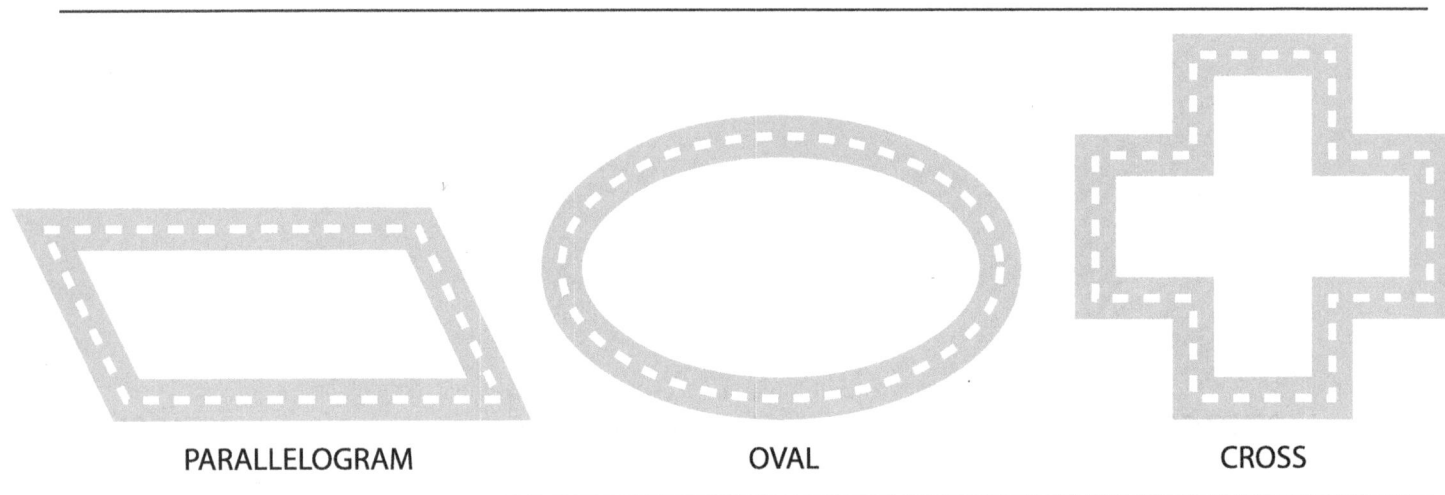

PARALLELOGRAM   OVAL   CROSS

Learn to Draw
Simple Shapes

Practice drawing simple shapes.
Trace on the dotted lines

HALF CIRCLE   HALF OVAL

Using the space below, practice drawing the shapes

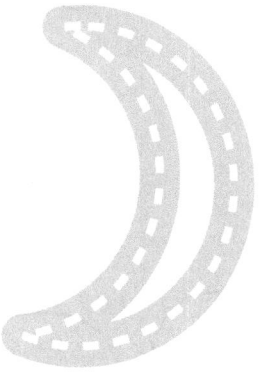

EGG   HEART   CRESCENT MOON

Lips

Eyes

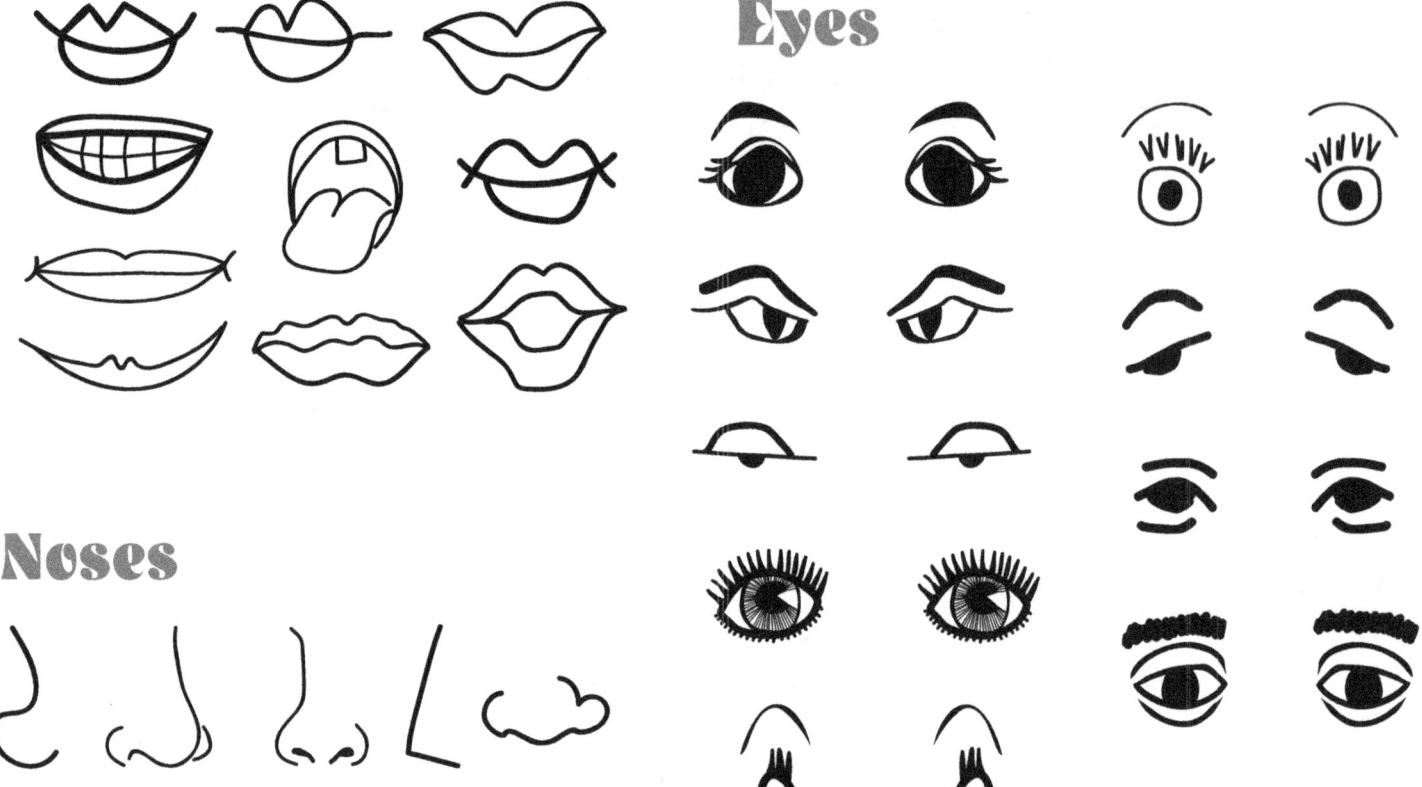

Noses

Hair Styles

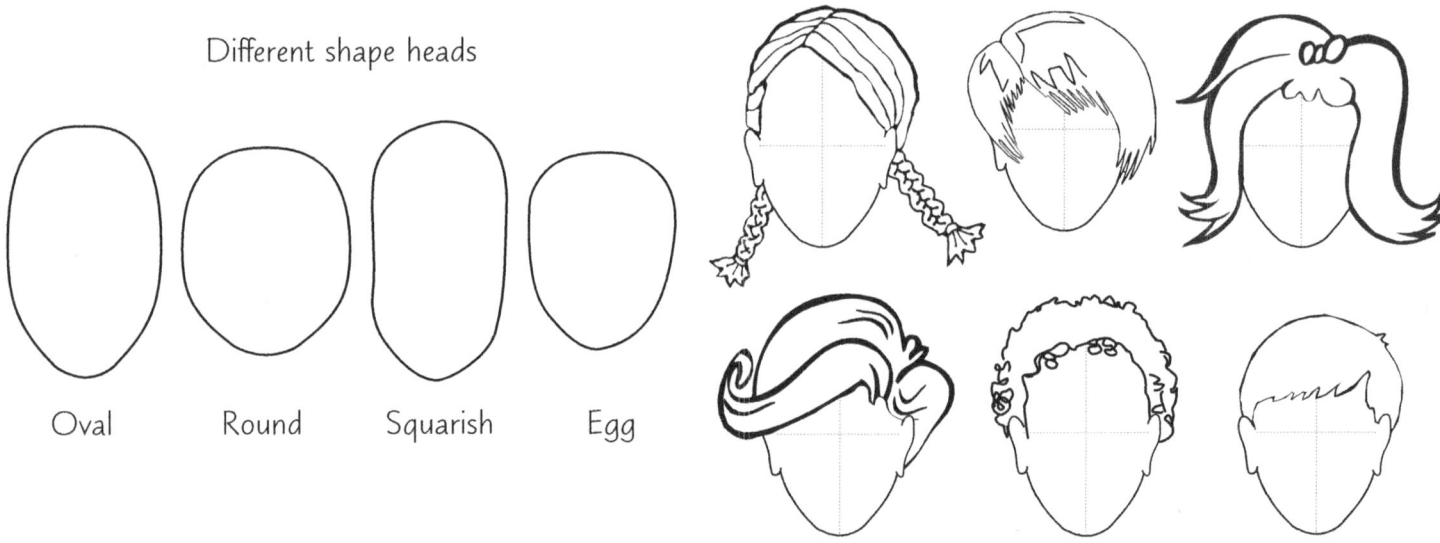

Different shape heads

Oval   Round   Squarish   Egg

Head Template

Photo copy or paste onto card stock and cut out
(use proper card stock for your printer)

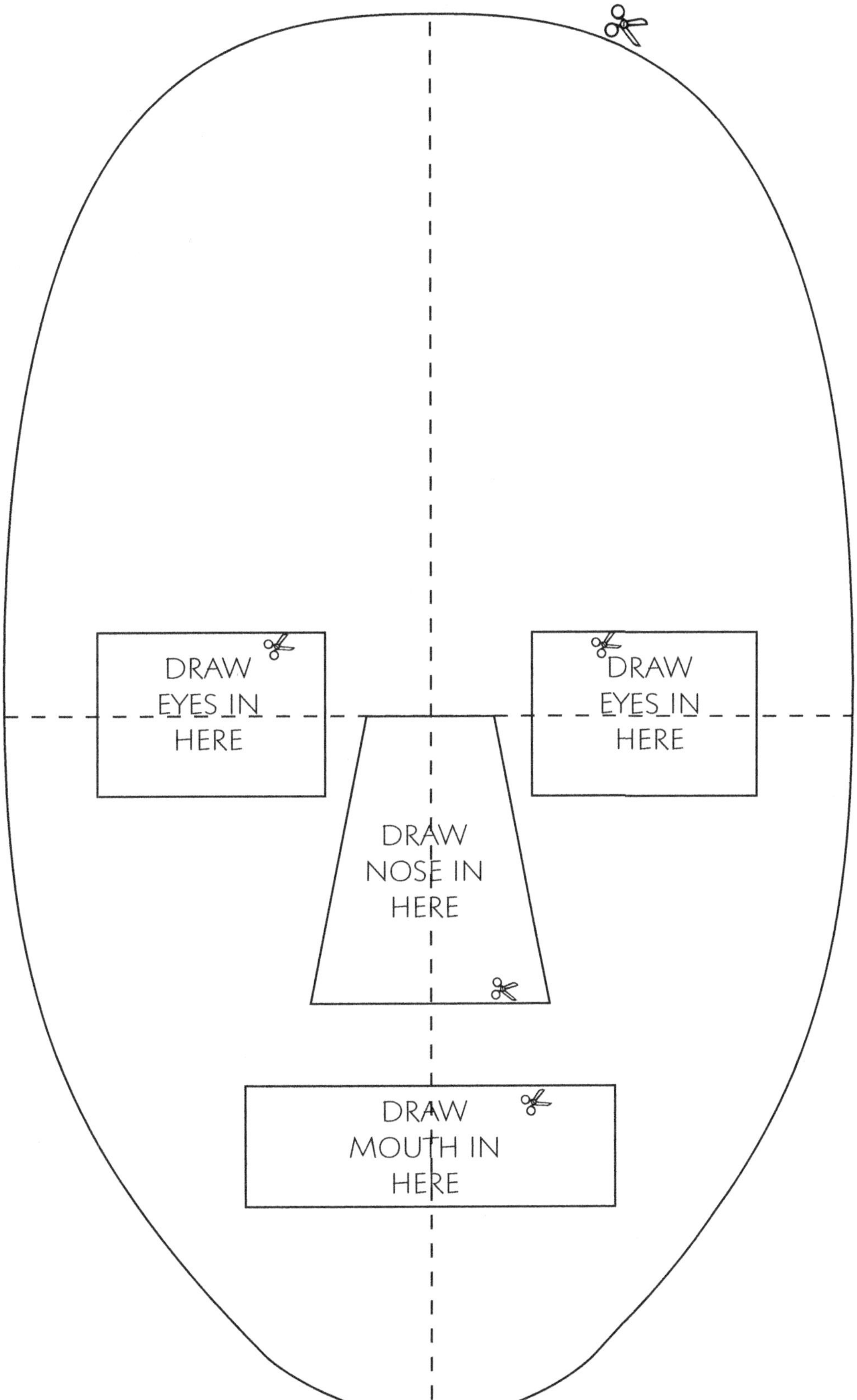

DRAW EYES IN HERE

DRAW EYES IN HERE

DRAW NOSE IN HERE

DRAW MOUTH IN HERE

Parents: Templates are good as a guide but sometimes they can restrict creativity. Encourage children to try drawing the face without the template first. I find children's face drawings are more expressive without the template and I only use it to get the general idea of proportion.

83

BACK OF HEAD TEMPLATE PAGE

BACK OF GRID A PAGE

Grid Templates

GRID A

Photocopy this onto transparency film for your printer

	A	B	C	D
1	1A	1B	1C	1D
2	2A	2B	2C	2D
3	3A	3B	3C	3D
4	4A	4B	4C	4D
5	5A	5B	5C	5D

Choose your own picture and place the transparency copy of this template over it. Transfer picture onto grid B. Look at page 55 for more instructions.

GRID B
Draw picture here

	A	B	C	D
1	1A	1B	1C	1D
2	2A	2B	2C	2D
3	3A	3B	3C	3D
4	4A	4B	4C	4D
5	5A	5B	5C	5D

You can either use this page in the book, cut it out, photocopy it, or print it online at:
www.chappythechipmonk.com/templates

GRID B
Draw picture here

	A	B	C	D
1	1A	1B	1C	1D
2	2A	2B	2C	2D
3	3A	3B	3C	3D
4	4A	4B	4C	4D
5	5A	5B	5C	5D

You can either use this page in the book, cut it out, photocopy it, or print it online at:
www.chappythechipmonk.com/templates

Make it Bigger

On the next pages you will transfer one smaller drawing to a bigger space. Many artist's use this technique. You can cut out your picture after you are done, and hang it on your wall.

Make it Bigger

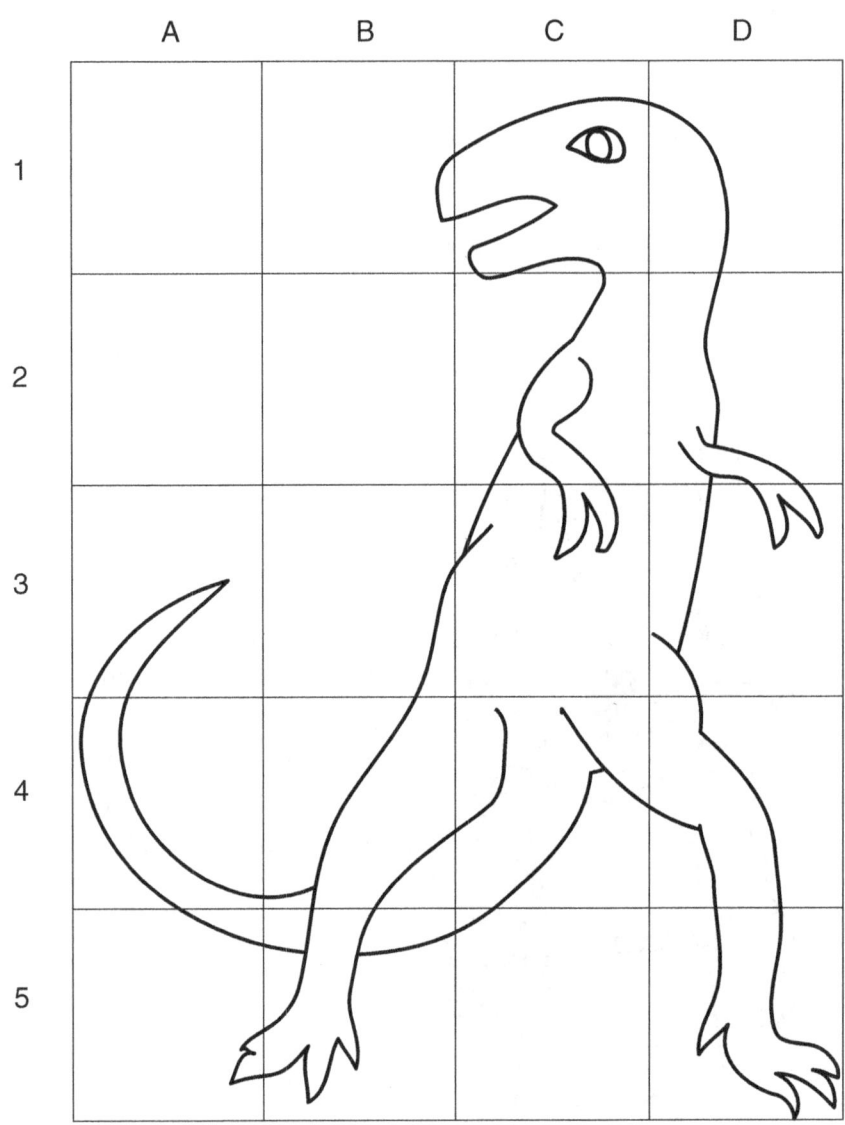

92

	A	B	C	D
1				
2				
3				
4				
5				

BACK OF MAKE IT BIGGER GRID PAGE

Make it Bigger
continued

Set your heart on doing good. Do it over and over again, and you will be filled with joy.

Make it bigger

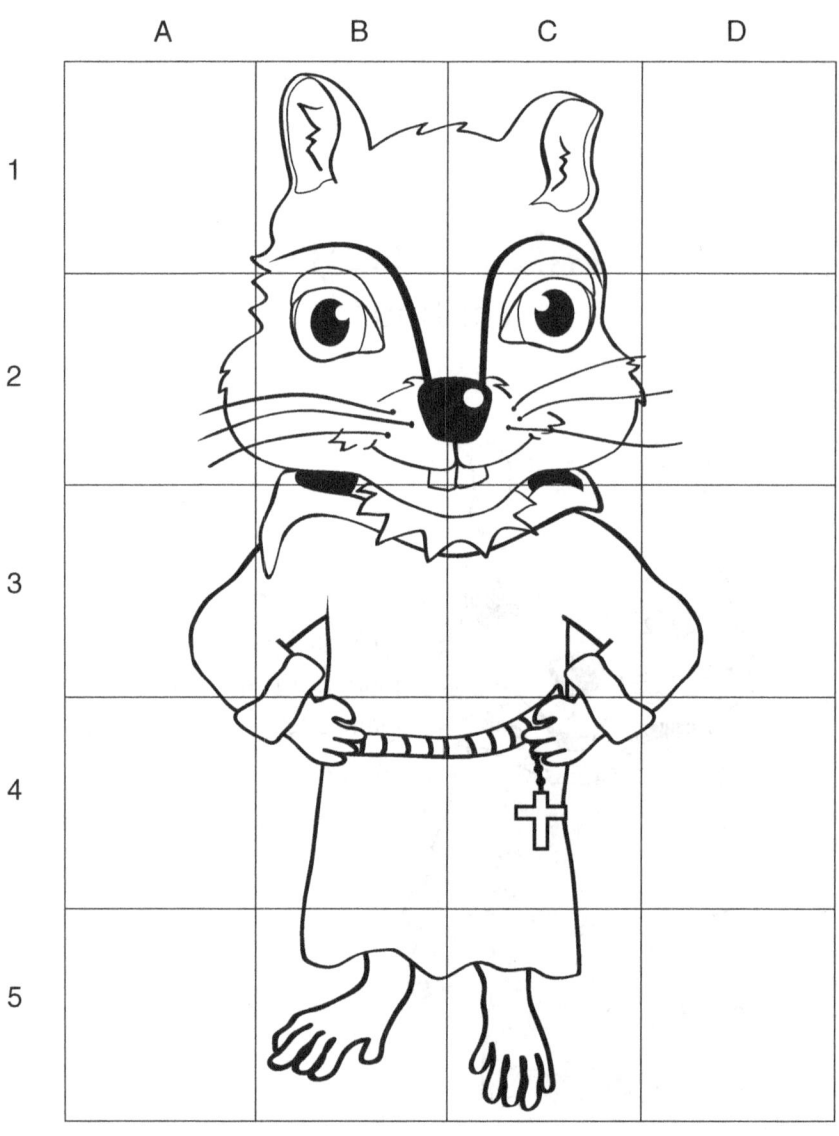

	A	B	C	D
1				
2				
3				
4				
5				

BACK OF MAKE IT BIGGER GRID PAGE

Chappy's Flash Card Shapes

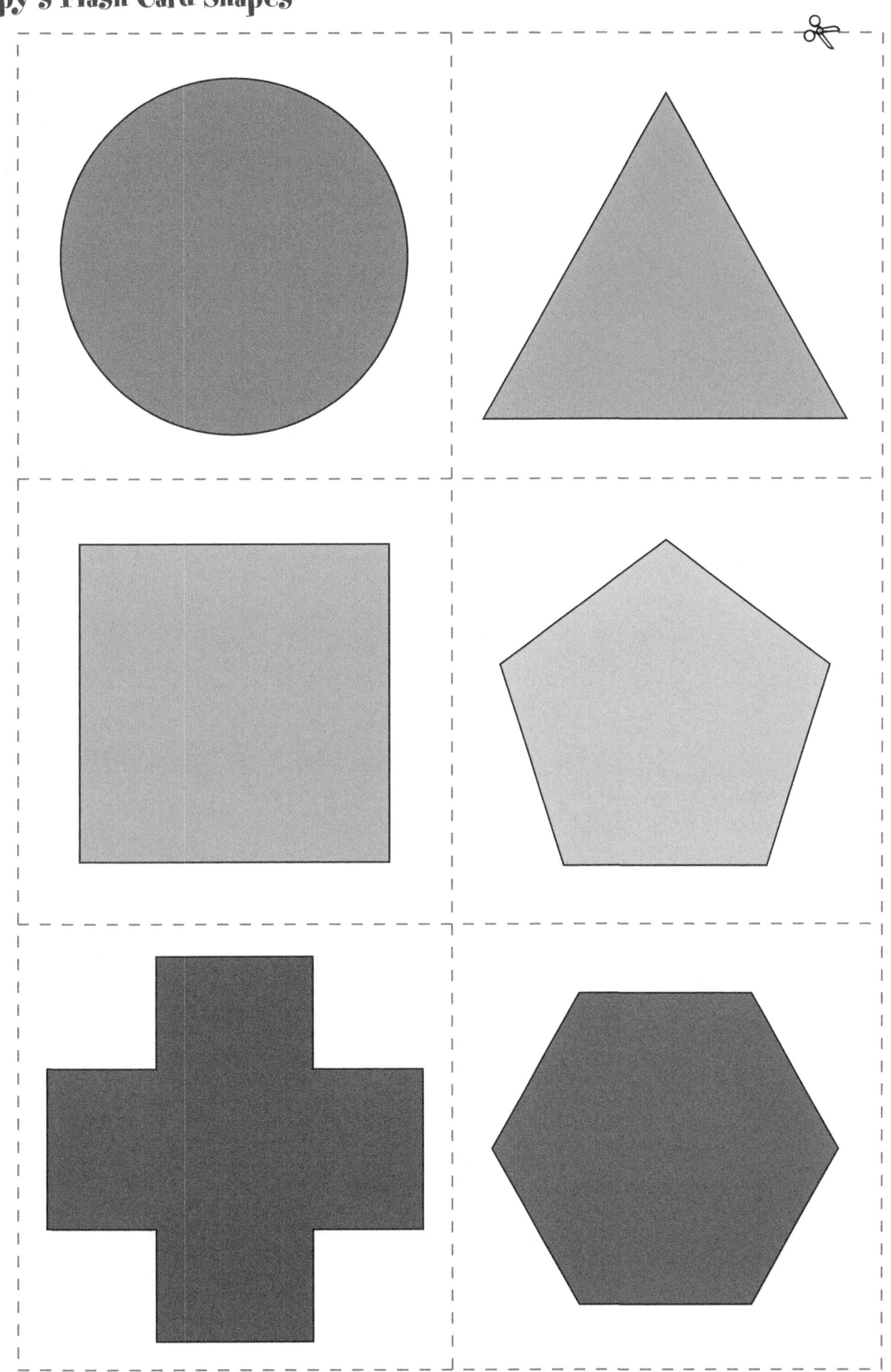

Also available online at: www.chappythechipmonk.com/templates

BACK OF FLASH CARD SHAPES PAGE

Chappy's Flash Card Shapes

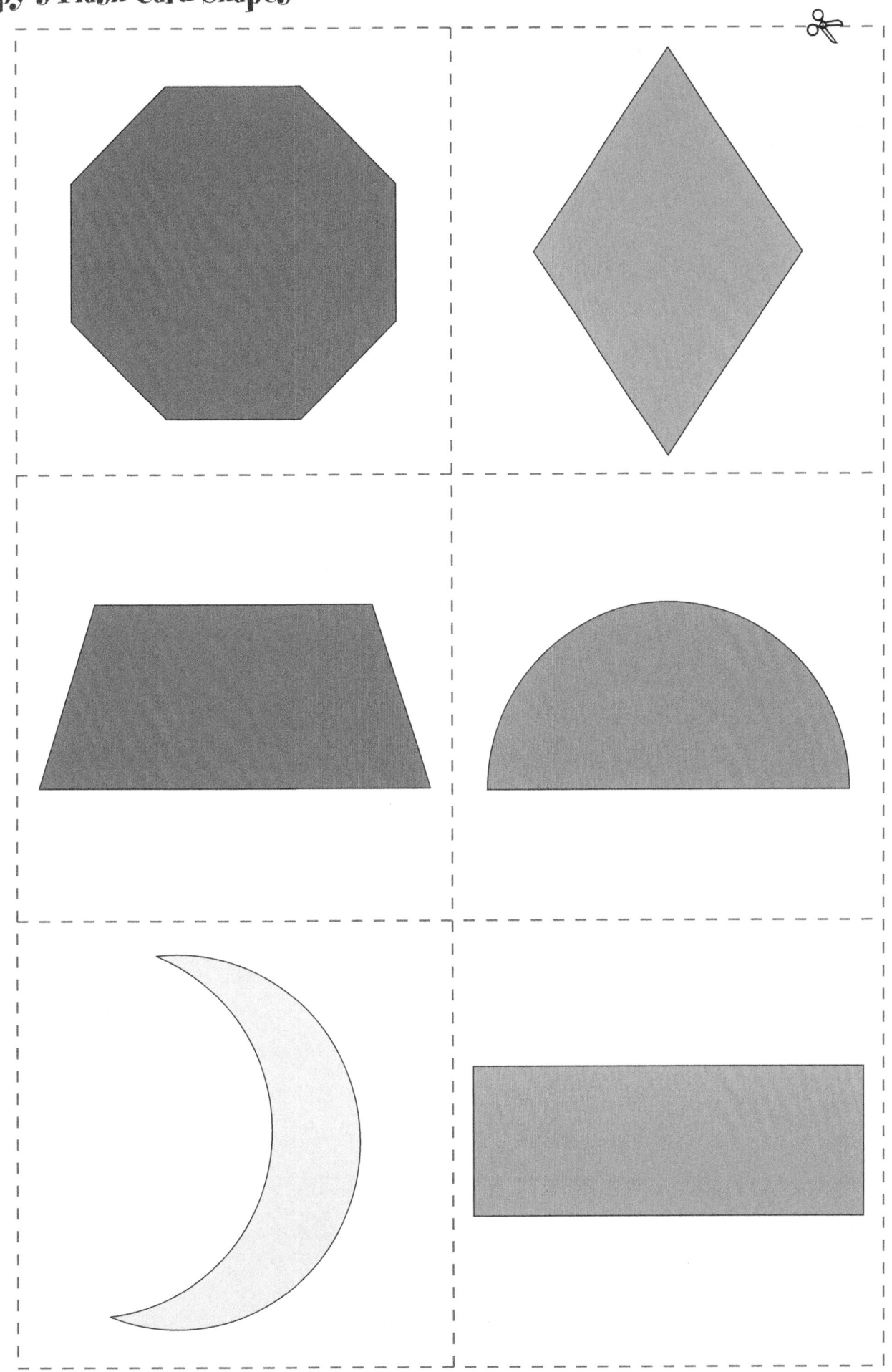

Also available online at: www.chappythechipmonk.com/templates

BACK OF FLASH CARD SHAPES PAGE

Chappy's Flash Card Shapes

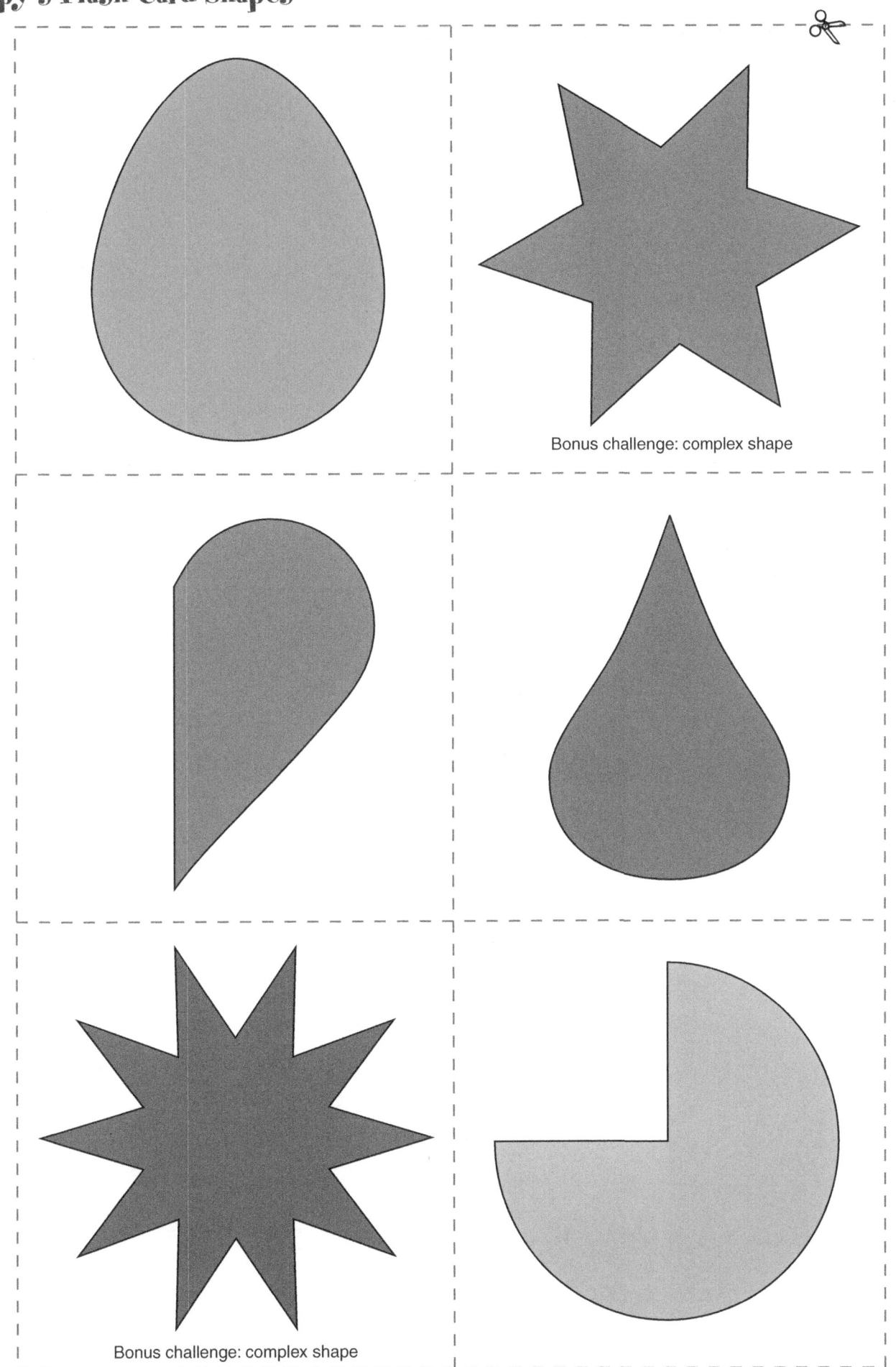

Bonus challenge: complex shape

Bonus challenge: complex shape

Also available online at: www.chappythechipmonk.com/templates

BACK OF FLASH CARD SHAPES PAGE

Chappy's Flash Card Blanks
Use this sheet to draw in shapes

Chappy's Flash Card Blanks

Also available online at: www.chappythechipmonk.com/templates

BACK OF FLASH CARD BLANKS PAGE

Chappy's Glossary

You will find, I use many words familiar with drawing that you may have never heard of, or you don't know their meaning. So, here's a list of them and there meanings.

Chappy's artistic word definitions used in the book:

Positive space: the shape of any object in a picture. A few examples are a ball, an ice ream cone, a person, a dinosaur, a chair, a face, a lamp. You get the idea.

Negative space: A shape that is behind, around or in between positive shapes in a picture.

Centered: in the middle

Symmetrical: The same on both sides

Proportional: A balanced relationship of parts to each other with regards to size.

Parallel: Lines extending in the same direction with equal space and not meeting.

Perpendicular: Any two lines that intersect each other at a ninety degree angle.

Horizontal: A line or object that is in a lying down position or when it is aligned in a "left-right" direction, parallel to the ground.

Vertical: A line or object that is standing up or when it is aligned in a "up - down" direction.

Angle: The figure formed by two lines extending from a point.

Template: A pattern used over and over again as a guide to help you draw.

About the Author

Michael Gugliotto was drawing at the early age of six. He remembers drawing an exact likeness of many cartoon characters such as, Bugs Bunny and Daffy Duck. Later as a teenager, his mother nurtured his talent by sending hime to a private art teacher by the name of Robert Hoffman. Robert Hoffman was an old master portrait painter who traveled all over the world and was commissioned by many royal families. During that time, Michael learned how to draw and paint portraits and was taught the master's unique methods.

Michael attended Munson Williams Proctor Art Institute where he continued to grow in his love for art. He received both a masters degree in printmaking, and a degree in art education. As a certified art teacher in the New York Public School System, he saw very few drawing books geared toward the elementary school aged child, and the ones he did see, he felt were written by grown ups who spent very little time with children. Most of the books were more for teenagers, that more than often, didn't work. He tested his *how to drawing methods* on elementary school children and on his own daughter and friends. If they didn't work he would re-think them, and try them another way until the children could grasp the concept.

Michael lives in Connecticut with his family.

Made in the USA
Las Vegas, NV
26 November 2024

12735864R00063